Pumpkin
Recipes

pil

Publications International, Ltd.

Let's get social!

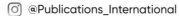 @Publications_International

 @PublicationsInternational

www.pilbooks.com

Table of Contents

Breakfast & Brunch

Chocolate Cranberry Pumpkin Pancakes

Makes 16 to 18 (4-inch) pancakes

2 cups all-purpose flour

⅓ cup packed brown sugar

2 teaspoons baking powder

½ teaspoon salt

½ teaspoon ground cinnamon

¼ teaspoon baking soda

¼ teaspoon ground ginger

¼ teaspoon ground nutmeg

1½ cups milk

2 eggs

½ cup canned pumpkin

¼ cup vegetable oil

½ cup mini semisweet chocolate chips

½ cup dried cranberries

⅓ cup cinnamon chips

1 to 2 teaspoons butter, plus additional for serving

Maple syrup

1. Combine flour, brown sugar, baking powder, salt, cinnamon, baking soda, ginger and nutmeg in large bowl; mix well.

2. Whisk milk, eggs, pumpkin and oil in medium bowl until well blended. Add to flour mixture with chocolate chips, cranberries and cinnamon chips; stir just until dry ingredients are moistened.

3. Heat 1 teaspoon butter on griddle over medium heat. Pour batter by ¼ cupfuls onto griddle. Cook until bubbles form and bottom of pancakes are lightly browned; turn and cook 2 minutes or until browned and cooked through. Repeat with remaining batter, adding additional butter to griddle if necessary. Serve pancakes with maple syrup and additional butter, if desired.

Pumpkin Streusel Coffeecake

Makes 9 servings

Streusel

½ cup all-purpose flour

½ cup packed brown sugar

2 teaspoons ground cinnamon

¼ cup (½ stick) butter, softened

½ cup chopped walnuts

Coffeecake

2 cups all-purpose flour

2 teaspoons baking powder

¾ teaspoon pumpkin pie spice

½ teaspoon baking soda

½ teaspoon salt

¾ cup packed brown sugar

½ cup (1 stick) butter, softened

2 eggs

1 cup canned pumpkin

2 teaspoons vanilla

1. Preheat oven to 325°F. Spray 8-inch square baking pan with nonstick cooking spray.

2. For streusel, combine ½ cup flour, ½ cup brown sugar and cinnamon in small bowl; mix well. Cut in ¼ cup butter with pastry blender or mix with fingertips until coarse crumbs form. Stir in walnuts. Refrigerate until ready to use.

3. For coffeecake, combine 2 cups flour, baking powder, pumpkin pie spice, baking soda and salt in medium bowl; mix well. Beat ¾ cup brown sugar and ½ cup butter in large bowl with electric mixer at medium-high speed until light and fluffy. Add eggs, one at a time, beating well at medium speed after each addition. Beat in pumpkin and vanilla until well blended. Add flour mixture; beat at low speed until blended. (Batter will be very thick.)

4. Spread half of batter in prepared pan; sprinkle with half of streusel. Top with remaining batter and streusel.

5. Bake about 40 minutes or until toothpick inserted into center comes out clean. Cool completely in pan on wire rack.

Pumpkin Waffles with Pumpkin Marmalade

Makes 10 waffles and 4 cups marmalade

1 can (29 ounces) pure pumpkin, divided

1 cup packed brown sugar

1 cup water

1 cup orange juice

1 tablespoon maple syrup

1 teaspoon finely grated orange peel

½ teaspoon ground ginger

¼ teaspoon salt

1 package (about 15 ounces) yellow cake mix

2 teaspoons pumpkin pie spice

1½ cups milk

2 eggs

¼ cup (½ stick) butter, melted

Whipped cream (optional)

1. Preheat oven to 200°F. Place wire rack on top of baking sheet; place in oven.

2. Reserve 1 cup pumpkin; set aside for waffles. Combine remaining pumpkin, brown sugar, water, orange juice, maple syrup, orange peel, ginger and salt in medium saucepan; bring to a simmer over medium heat. Cook until mixture thickens to consistency of applesauce, stirring occasionally. Reduce heat to low; keep warm.

3. Combine cake mix and pumpkin pie spice in large bowl; mix well. Whisk milk, reserved 1 cup pumpkin, eggs and butter in medium bowl until well blended. Add to dry ingredients; stir until blended.

4. Preheat waffle iron according to manufacturer's directions. Spray cooking surface with nonstick cooking spray.

5. Pour ½ cup batter into heated waffle iron. Cook until steaming stops and waffle is lightly browned and crisp. Remove to wire rack in oven to keep warm. Repeat with remaining batter. Serve with warm pumpkin marmalade and whipped cream, if desired. Refrigerate leftover marmalade.

Tip: Serve leftover pumpkin marmalade on toast or with bagels and cream cheese.

Cinnamon-Sugared Pumpkin Pecan Muffins

Makes 1 dozen muffins

8 tablespoons sugar, divided

2½ teaspoons ground cinnamon, divided

1 cup 100% bran cereal

1 cup milk

1 cup all-purpose flour

1 tablespoon baking powder

½ teaspoon baking soda

½ teaspoon salt

1 cup canned pumpkin

1 egg, beaten

1 tablespoon vanilla

1 package (2 ounces) pecan chips (½ cup)

1. Preheat oven to 400°F. Spray 12 standard (2½-inch) nonstick muffin cups with nonstick cooking spray. Combine 2 tablespoons sugar and ½ teaspoon cinnamon in small bowl; mix well.

2. Combine cereal and milk in large bowl; let stand 5 minutes to soften. Combine flour, remaining 6 tablespoons sugar, 2 teaspoons cinnamon, baking powder, baking soda and salt in large bowl; mix well.

3. Whisk pumpkin, egg and vanilla into cereal mixture until well blended. Add flour mixture; stir just until blended. *Do not overmix.* Spoon batter evenly into prepared muffin cups; sprinkle with pecan chips and cinnamon-sugar.

4. Bake 20 to 25 minutes or until toothpick inserted into centers comes out clean. Cool in pan 3 minutes; remove to wire rack. Serve warm or at room temperature.

Pumpkin Power Smoothie >>

Makes 1 serving

⅓ cup water

1 sweet red apple, seeded and cut into chunks

½ frozen banana

½ cup canned pumpkin

½ cup ice cubes

1 tablespoon lemon juice

1 tablespoon ground flaxseed

1 teaspoon honey

Dash ground nutmeg

Combine water, apple, banana, pumpkin, ice, lemon juice, flaxseed, honey and nutmeg in blender; blend until smooth. Serve immediately.

Spiced Pumpkin Banana Smoothie

Makes 1 serving

½ cup almond milk

½ frozen banana

½ cup canned pumpkin

½ cup ice cubes

1 tablespoon honey

¼ teaspoon ground cinnamon

⅛ teaspoon ground ginger

Dash ground nutmeg

Combine almond milk, banana, pumpkin, ice, honey, cinnamon, ginger and nutmeg in blender; blend until smooth. Serve immediately.

Pumpkin Spice Mini Doughnuts

Makes 3 dozen doughnuts

½ cup granulated sugar

4 teaspoons ground cinnamon, divided

2 cups all-purpose flour

½ cup packed brown sugar

1½ teaspoons baking powder

½ teaspoon salt

½ teaspoon ground ginger

½ teaspoon ground nutmeg

¼ teaspoon baking soda

2 eggs

½ cup canned pumpkin

¼ cup (½ stick) butter, softened

¼ cup milk

1 teaspoon vanilla

¼ cup (½ stick) butter, melted

1. Preheat oven to 350°F. Spray 36 mini (1¾-inch) muffin cups with nonstick cooking spray. Combine granulated sugar and 3 teaspoons cinnamon in shallow bowl; set aside.

2. Combine flour, brown sugar, baking powder, remaining 1 teaspoon cinnamon, salt, ginger, nutmeg and baking soda in medium bowl; mix well. Beat eggs, pumpkin, softened butter, milk and vanilla in large bowl with electric mixer at medium speed until well blended. Gradually add flour mixture; beat just until blended. Spoon scant tablespoonful batter into each prepared muffin cup.

3. Bake 12 minutes or until toothpick inserted into centers comes out clean. Cool in pans 2 minutes.

4. Working with one doughnut at a time, brush all over with melted butter and roll in cinnamon-sugar to coat. Return to wire racks to cool slightly. Serve warm or cool completely.

Baked Pumpkin Oatmeal

Makes 6 servings

2 cups old-fashioned oats

2 cups milk

1 cup canned pumpkin

2 eggs

⅓ cup packed brown sugar

1 teaspoon vanilla

½ cup dried cranberries, plus additional for topping

1 teaspoon pumpkin pie spice

½ teaspoon salt

½ teaspoon baking powder

Maple syrup

Chopped pecans (optional)

1. Preheat oven to 350°F. Spray 8-inch square baking dish with nonstick cooking spray.

2. Spread oats on ungreased baking sheet. Bake 10 minutes or until fragrant and lightly browned, stirring occasionally. Pour into medium bowl; let cool slightly.

3. Whisk milk, pumpkin, eggs, brown sugar and vanilla in large bowl until well blended. Add ½ cup cranberries, pumpkin pie spice, salt and baking powder to oats; mix well. Add oat mixture to pumpkin mixture; stir until well blended. Pour into prepared baking dish.

4. Bake 45 minutes or until set and knife inserted into center comes out almost clean. Serve warm with maple syrup, additional cranberries and pecans, if desired.

Baked Pumpkin Bites

Makes 2 dozen mini muffins

¾ cup canned pumpkin

½ cup milk

½ cup packed brown sugar

⅓ cup vegetable oil

1 egg

1 teaspoon vanilla

1¾ cups all-purpose flour

2 teaspoons baking powder

2 teaspoons ground cinnamon, divided

½ teaspoon ground nutmeg

½ teaspoon salt

1 cup powdered sugar

⅓ cup maple syrup

¼ cup granulated sugar

1. Preheat oven to 350°F. Spray 24 mini (1¾-inch) muffin cups with nonstick cooking spray.

2. Whisk pumpkin, milk, brown sugar, oil, egg and vanilla in large bowl until well blended. Add flour, baking powder, 1 teaspoon cinnamon, nutmeg and salt; stir just until combined. Spoon heaping tablespoonful batter into each prepared muffin cup.

3. Bake 12 minutes or until toothpick inserted into centers comes out clean. Cool in pans 5 minutes; remove to wire rack.

4. Combine powdered sugar and maple syrup in small bowl; microwave on HIGH 30 seconds. Stir until well blended and smooth. Combine granulated sugar and remaining 1 teaspoon cinnamon in small bowl.

5. Dip tops of muffins into glaze; sprinkle lightly with cinnamon-sugar.

Pumpkin Cinnamon Rolls

Makes 12 rolls

Dough

- ½ cup milk
- ¼ cup (½ stick) butter
- 1 package (¼ ounce) rapid-rise yeast
- ⅔ cup canned pumpkin
- ½ cup packed brown sugar
- 1 egg
- 1 teaspoon salt
- ½ teaspoon pumpkin pie spice
- 3½ to 4 cups all-purpose flour

Filling

- ¾ cup packed brown sugar
- 2 teaspoons ground cinnamon
- Pinch salt
- ¼ cup (½ stick) butter, softened

Glaze

- 1 cup powdered sugar
- 2 ounces cream cheese, softened
- 1 to 2 tablespoons milk
- ½ teaspoon vanilla

1. Heat milk and ¼ cup butter to 120°F in small microwavable bowl. Stir in yeast; let stand 5 minutes or until mixture is bubbly.

2. Combine pumpkin, ½ cup brown sugar, egg, 1 teaspoon salt, pumpkin pie spice and milk mixture in large bowl of stand mixer; beat at low speed until well blended. Add 3½ cups flour; knead with dough hook at low speed 5 minutes or until dough is smooth and elastic, adding additional flour by tablespoonfuls if necessary.

3. Shape dough into a ball. Place in large greased bowl; turn to grease top. Cover and let rise in warm place 1 hour 15 minutes or until doubled in size.

4. Spray 13×9-inch baking pan with nonstick cooking spray. Combine ¾ cup brown sugar, cinnamon and pinch of salt in small bowl; mix well. Punch down dough; roll out into 18×14-inch rectangle on lightly floured surface. Spread ¼ cup softened butter over dough; sprinkle with brown sugar mixture. Starting with long end, roll up dough tightly jelly-roll style; pinch seam to seal. Trim ends; cut roll crosswise into 12 slices. Place slices cut sides up in prepared pan. Cover and let rise in warm place 45 minutes or until almost doubled in size. Preheat oven to 350°F.

5. Bake about 20 minutes or until lightly browned. Meanwhile, whisk powdered sugar, cream cheese, 1 tablespoon milk and vanilla in medium bowl until smooth. Add remaining 1 tablespoon milk to thin glaze, if desired. Drizzle over warm rolls.

Pumpkin Granola

Makes about 5½ cups

3 cups old-fashioned oats

¾ cup coarsely chopped almonds

¾ cup raw pumpkin seeds

½ cup canned pumpkin

½ cup maple syrup

⅓ cup coconut oil, melted

1 teaspoon vanilla

1 teaspoon ground cinnamon

½ teaspoon salt

¼ teaspoon ground ginger

¼ teaspoon ground nutmeg

Pinch ground cloves

¾ cup dried cranberries

1. Preheat oven to 325°F. Line large rimmed baking sheet with parchment paper.

2. Combine oats, almonds and pumpkin seeds in large bowl; mix well. Whisk pumpkin, maple syrup, oil, vanilla, cinnamon, salt, ginger, nutmeg and cloves in medium bowl until well blended. Pour over oat mixture; stir until well blended and all ingredients are completely coated. Spread evenly on prepared baking sheet.

3. Bake 50 to 60 minutes or until granola is golden brown and no longer moist, stirring every 20 minutes. (Granola will become more crisp as it cools.) Stir in cranberries; cool completely.

Variations: For Pumpkin Chocolate Granola, follow the recipe above but reduce the amount of maple syrup to ⅓ cup. Stir in ¾ cup semisweet chocolate chips after baking. You can substitute pecans or walnuts for the almonds, and/or add ¾ cup flaked coconut to the mixture before baking.

Pumpkin Spice Doughnuts

Makes 14 to 16 doughnuts

2¾ cups all-purpose flour

¼ cup cornstarch

2 teaspoons pumpkin pie spice

1¼ teaspoons baking powder

1 teaspoon salt

½ teaspoon baking soda

1 cup granulated sugar

2 eggs

¼ cup (½ stick) butter, melted

¼ cup canned pumpkin

1 teaspoon vanilla

½ cup buttermilk

Vegetable oil for frying

Caramel Glaze

½ cup packed brown sugar

1 tablespoon butter

2 tablespoons whipping cream, divided

Coarse salt (optional)

1. Combine flour, cornstarch, pumpkin pie spice, baking powder, salt and baking soda in large bowl.

2. Beat granulated sugar and eggs in large bowl with electric mixer at high speed 3 minutes or until pale and thick. Beat in ¼ cup melted butter, pumpkin and vanilla at low speed until blended. Add flour mixture alternately with buttermilk, beating at low speed until blended after each addition. Press plastic wrap directly onto surface of dough; refrigerate at least 1 hour.

3. Pour about 2 inches of oil into Dutch oven or large heavy saucepan; clip deep-fry or candy thermometer to side of pan. Heat oil over medium-high heat to 360°F to 370°F.

4. Meanwhile, generously flour work surface. Turn out dough onto work surface and dust top with flour. Roll dough to ¼-inch thickness. Cut out doughnuts with floured doughnut cutter; gather and reroll scraps. Line large wire rack with paper towels.

5. Working in batches, add doughnuts to hot oil. (Do not crowd pan.) Cook 1 minute per side or until golden brown, adjusting heat to maintain temperature during frying. Cool on wire rack.

6. For glaze, combine brown sugar, 1 tablespoon butter and 1 tablespoon cream in small saucepan; bring to a boil over medium-high heat. Boil 2 minutes. Remove from heat; stir in remaining 1 tablespoon cream. Working quickly, drizzle glaze over doughnuts and holes. Sprinkle with coarse salt, if desired.

Cranberry Pumpkin Nut Bread

Makes 1 loaf

2 cups all-purpose flour

2 teaspoons pumpkin pie spice

1 teaspoon baking powder

½ teaspoon baking soda

½ teaspoon salt

1 cup canned pumpkin

¾ cup granulated sugar

½ cup packed brown sugar

2 eggs

⅓ cup vegetable or canola oil

1 cup chopped dried cranberries

¾ cup chopped macadamia nuts, toasted*

To toast macadamia nuts, spread on baking sheet. Bake in 350°F oven 8 to 10 minutes or until lightly browned, stirring occasionally.

1. Preheat oven to 350°F. Spray 9×5-inch loaf pan with nonstick cooking spray.

2. Combine flour, pumpkin pie spice, baking powder, baking soda and salt in large bowl; mix well. Whisk pumpkin, granulated sugar, brown sugar, eggs and oil in medium bowl until well blended. Add to flour mixture; stir just until dry ingredients are moistened. Stir in cranberries and nuts. Pour batter into prepared pan.

3. Bake 45 to 50 minutes or until toothpick inserted into center comes out clean. Cool in pan 15 minutes; remove to wire rack to cool completely.

Pumpkin Spice Latte

Makes 2 servings

1¾ cups milk, divided

½ cup canned pumpkin

3 tablespoons packed brown sugar

1 teaspoon grated fresh ginger

1 teaspoon pumpkin pie spice

½ teaspoon ground cinnamon, plus additional for garnish

¼ teaspoon salt

⅛ teaspoon coarsely ground black pepper

1 cup strong-brewed hot coffee*

1 tablespoon vanilla

Whipped cream (optional)

Use about 1 tablespoon ground espresso roast or other dark roast coffee for each 3 ounces of water.

1. Combine ½ cup milk, pumpkin, brown sugar, ginger, pumpkin pie spice, ½ teaspoon cinnamon, salt and pepper in medium saucepan; whisk until well blended. Cook over medium-low heat 10 minutes, whisking frequently.

2. Remove from heat; whisk in coffee and vanilla. Strain through fine-mesh strainer into medium bowl.

3. Bring remaining 1¼ cups milk to a simmer in small saucepan over medium-high heat. For froth, whisk vigorously 30 seconds. Whisk into coffee mixture until blended. Pour into two mugs; garnish with whipped cream and additional cinnamon.

Maple Pumpkin Butter

Makes 4 cups

2 cans (15 ounces each) pure pumpkin

¾ cup packed dark brown sugar

¼ cup maple syrup

2 teaspoons ground cinnamon

½ teaspoon ground ginger

¼ teaspoon ground cloves

¼ teaspoon ground allspice

¼ teaspoon ground nutmeg

⅛ teaspoon salt

1 tablespoon lemon juice

Slow Cooker Directions

1. Combine pumpkin, brown sugar, maple syrup, cinnamon, ginger, cloves, allspice, nutmeg and salt in slow cooker; mix well.

2. Cover; cook on LOW 7 hours, stirring every 2 to 3 hours.

3. Stir in lemon juice. Transfer pumpkin butter to storage containers; cool completely. Cover and refrigerate up to 3 weeks.

Pumpkin Ginger Scones

Makes 1 dozen scones

½ cup sugar, divided

2 cups all-purpose flour

2 teaspoons baking powder

1 teaspoon ground cinnamon

½ teaspoon baking soda

½ teaspoon salt

¼ cup (½ stick) cold butter, cut into small pieces

1 egg

½ cup canned pumpkin

¼ cup sour cream

½ teaspoon grated fresh ginger *or* 2 tablespoons finely chopped crystallized ginger

1 tablespoon butter, melted

1. Preheat oven to 425°F.

2. Reserve 1 tablespoon sugar; set aside. Combine remaining sugar, flour, baking powder, cinnamon, baking soda and salt in large bowl. Cut in ¼ cup cold butter with pastry blender or two knives until mixture resembles coarse crumbs.

3. Beat egg in medium bowl. Add pumpkin, sour cream and ginger; beat until well blended. Add to flour mixture; stir to form soft dough that leaves side of bowl.

4. Turn out dough onto well-floured surface; knead 10 times. Roll out dough into 9×6-inch rectangle with floured rolling pin. Cut into six 3-inch squares; cut each square diagonally in half to make 12 triangles. Place 2 inches apart on ungreased baking sheets. Brush tops with 1 tablespoon melted butter; sprinkle with reserved sugar.

5. Bake 10 to 12 minutes or until golden brown. Remove to wire racks to cool 10 minutes. Serve warm.

Baked Pumpkin French Toast

Makes 6 servings

1 tablespoon butter, softened

1 loaf challah or egg bread (12 to 16 ounces), cut into ¾-inch-thick slices

7 eggs

1¼ cups whole milk

⅔ cup canned pumpkin

1 teaspoon vanilla

½ teaspoon pumpkin pie spice

⅛ teaspoon salt

3 tablespoons sugar

2 teaspoons ground cinnamon

Maple syrup

1. Generously grease 13×9-inch baking dish with butter. Arrange bread slices in dish, fitting slices in tightly.

2. Whisk eggs, milk, pumpkin, vanilla, pumpkin pie spice and salt in medium bowl until well blended. Pour over bread in prepared baking dish; turn slices to coat completely. Cover and refrigerate 8 hours or overnight.

3. Preheat oven to 350°F. Combine sugar and cinnamon in small bowl; mix well. Turn bread slices again; sprinkle generously with cinnamon-sugar.

4. Bake 30 minutes or until bread is puffy and golden brown. Serve immediately with maple syrup.

Savory Pumpkin

Pumpkin Parmesan Twice-Baked Potatoes

Makes 4 servings

2 baking potatoes
(about 12 ounces each)

1 cup shredded Parmesan
cheese

6 tablespoons half-and-half

¼ cup canned pumpkin

1½ teaspoons minced fresh sage
or ¼ teaspoon dried thyme

¼ teaspoon salt

⅛ teaspoon black pepper

1. Preheat oven to 400°F. Scrub potatoes; pierce in several places with fork or small knife. Place potatoes directly on oven rack; bake 1 hour or until soft.

2. When cool enough to handle, cut potatoes in half lengthwise. Scoop out most of potato pulp into medium bowl, leaving thin potato shell. Mash potatoes with fork. Add cheese, half-and-half, pumpkin, sage, salt and pepper; mix well.

3. Place potato shells on baking sheet; spoon pumpkin mixture into shells. Bake 10 minutes or until filling is heated through.

Pumpkin and Roasted Pepper Soup

Makes 6 servings

2 tablespoons butter

1 red onion, chopped

1 stalk celery, chopped

3 cups chicken broth

1 can (15 ounces) pure pumpkin

½ cup chopped roasted
   red pepper

½ teaspoon salt

½ teaspoon paprika

¼ teaspoon dried thyme

¼ teaspoon black pepper

2 tablespoons half-and-half

1. Melt butter in large saucepan over medium-high heat. Add onion and celery; cook 5 minutes or until onion is translucent, stirring occasionally.

2. Add broth, pumpkin, roasted pepper, salt, paprika, thyme and black pepper; bring to a boil. Reduce heat to low; cook 30 minutes, stirring occasionally.

3. Working in batches, process soup in food processor or blender until smooth. (Or use hand-held immersion blender.) Return soup to saucepan; stir in half-and-half. Cook until heated through, stirring occasionally.

Pumpkin Risotto

Makes 4 servings

4 cups (32 ounces) vegetable broth

5 whole fresh sage leaves

¼ teaspoon ground nutmeg

2 tablespoons butter

1 tablespoon olive oil

1 onion, finely chopped

2 cloves garlic, minced

1½ cups uncooked arborio rice

½ cup dry white wine

1 teaspoon salt

Black pepper

1 can (15 ounces) pure pumpkin

½ cup shredded Parmesan cheese

2 tablespoons chopped fresh sage, divided

¼ cup roasted pumpkin seeds or chopped toasted walnuts or pecans

1. Combine broth, whole sage leaves and nutmeg in small saucepan; bring to a boil over high heat. Reduce heat to low to maintain a simmer.

2. Heat butter and oil in large saucepan over medium-high heat. Add onion; cook and stir 5 minutes or until softened. Add garlic; cook and stir 30 seconds. Add rice; cook 2 to 3 minutes or until rice appears translucent, stirring frequently to coat with butter. Add wine, salt and pepper; cook until most of liquid is absorbed.

3. Add broth mixture to saucepan with rice mixture, ½ cup at a time, stirring frequently until broth is absorbed before adding next ½ cup (discard whole sage leaves). Stir in pumpkin when about 1 cup broth remains. Add remaining broth; cook until rice is al dente, stirring constantly.

4. Remove from heat; stir in cheese and 1 tablespoon chopped sage. Cover and let stand 5 minutes. Top each serving with 1 tablespoon pumpkin seeds and remaining chopped sage.

Sweet Onion Pumpkin Seed Focaccia

Makes 10 servings

1 package (about 14 ounces) refrigerated pizza dough

¼ cup olive oil

2 red onions, thinly sliced

¼ cup raw pumpkin seeds

½ teaspoon dried oregano

¼ teaspoon salt

⅛ teaspoon red pepper flakes

⅛ teaspoon black pepper

1. Preheat oven to 400°F. Line jelly-roll pan or large baking sheet with parchment paper or spray with nonstick cooking spray.

2. Unroll dough on prepared baking pan; press into 15×10-inch rectangle. Bake 10 minutes.

3. Meanwhile, heat oil in large skillet over medium-high heat. Add onions; cook and stir 7 minutes or until tender. Add pumpkin seeds, oregano, salt, red pepper flakes and black pepper; cook and stir 3 minutes. Spread onion mixture evenly over partially baked crust.

4. Bake 10 to 14 minutes or until crust is golden and onions begin to brown. Let stand 5 minutes before cutting.

Creamy Pumpkin Baked Penne

Makes 6 to 8 servings

1 package (about 14 ounces) uncooked multigrain penne pasta

1 tablespoon olive oil

1 small onion, chopped

3 cloves garlic, minced

1 can (28 ounces) crushed tomatoes

1 can (15 ounces) pure pumpkin

¾ cup ricotta cheese

½ cup chicken broth

1 tablespoon Italian seasoning

½ teaspoon red pepper flakes

1 cup (4 ounces) shredded mozzarella cheese

⅓ cup grated Parmesan cheese

1. Preheat oven to 375°F. Spray 13×9-inch baking dish with nonstick cooking spray.

2. Cook pasta according to package directions until al dente.

3. Meanwhile, heat oil in large saucepan or Dutch oven over medium-high heat. Add onion and garlic; cook and stir 3 minutes. Add tomatoes, pumpkin, ricotta, broth, Italian seasoning and red pepper flakes; bring to a boil. Reduce heat to medium-low; cook 5 minutes, stirring occasionally. Add pasta; stir until coated with sauce. Spoon into prepared baking dish; sprinkle with mozzarella and Parmesan.

4. Bake 30 to 35 minutes or until cheeses are melted and beginning to brown.

Spicy Pumpkin Soup

Makes 8 to 10 servings

2 teaspoons olive oil

½ cup raw pumpkin seeds

1 onion, chopped

1 teaspoon coarse salt

¾ teaspoon chipotle
    chili powder

½ teaspoon black pepper

2 cans (29 ounces each)
    pure pumpkin

4 cups chicken broth

¾ cup apple cider

½ cup whipping cream
    Sour cream (optional)

3 slices thick-cut bacon,
    crisp-cooked and crumbled

Slow Cooker Directions

1. Heat oil in medium skillet over medium heat. Add pumpkin seeds; cook and stir about 1 minute or until seeds begin to pop. Remove to small bowl; set aside.

2. Add onion to same skillet; cook and stir over medium heat until translucent. Stir in salt, chipotle powder and black pepper. Transfer to slow cooker. Stir in pumpkin, broth and cider until well blended.

3. Cover; cook on HIGH 4 hours. Turn off slow cooker. Stir in cream until blended.

4. Strain soup for smoother texture, if desired. Garnish with sour cream, toasted pumpkin seeds and bacon.

Savory Pumpkin Hummus

Makes 1½ cups (about 12 servings)

1 can (15 ounces) pure pumpkin

3 tablespoons chopped fresh parsley, plus additional for garnish

3 tablespoons tahini

3 tablespoons lemon juice

3 cloves garlic

1 teaspoon ground cumin

½ teaspoon salt

⅛ teaspoon black pepper

⅛ teaspoon ground red pepper, plus additional for garnish

Assorted vegetable sticks

1. Combine pumpkin, 3 tablespoons parsley, tahini, lemon juice, garlic, cumin, salt, black pepper and ⅛ teaspoon red pepper in food processor or blender; process until smooth. Cover and refrigerate at least 2 hours to allow flavors to develop.

2. Garnish with additional parsley and red pepper. Serve with assorted vegetable sticks.

Pumpkin Polenta

Makes 4 servings

1 tablespoon olive oil

1 tablespoon butter, plus
    additional for serving

1 medium onion, chopped

½ teaspoon smoked paprika

½ teaspoon salt

¼ teaspoon ground mace
    or nutmeg

⅛ teaspoon ground red pepper

1 can (15 ounces) pure pumpkin

2 cups vegetable broth or water

1 cup milk

1 cup instant polenta

½ cup (2 ounces) shredded
    fontina cheese, plus
    additional for serving

Fresh thyme (optional)

1. Heat oil and 1 tablespoon butter in medium saucepan over medium heat. Add onion; cook and stir 5 minutes or until softened. Add paprika, salt, mace and red pepper; cook 30 seconds, stirring constantly. Add pumpkin; cook 2 minutes, stirring frequently.

2. Whisk in broth and milk; bring to a boil over high heat. Stir in polenta in thin, steady stream. Reduce heat to medium-high; cook 5 minutes or until very thick, stirring constantly.

3. Remove from heat; stir in ½ cup cheese until melted. Top each serving with additional butter and cheese, if desired. Garnish with thyme.

Curried Ginger Pumpkin Soup

Makes 8 servings

1 tablespoon vegetable oil

1 large sweet onion (such as Walla Walla), coarsely chopped

1 large Golden Delicious apple, peeled and coarsely chopped

3 (¼-inch) slices peeled fresh ginger

1½ teaspoons curry powder

2½ to 3 cups chicken broth, divided

2 cans (15 ounces each) pure pumpkin

1 cup half-and-half

1 teaspoon salt

¼ teaspoon black pepper

Roasted salted pumpkin seeds (optional)

1. Heat oil in large saucepan over medium heat. Add onion, apple, ginger and curry powder; cook 10 minutes, stirring occasionally. Add ½ cup broth; cover and cook 10 minutes or until apple is tender.

2. Pour onion mixture into blender; blend until smooth. (Or use hand-held immersion blender.) Return to saucepan.

3. Stir in pumpkin, 2 cups broth, half-and-half, salt and pepper; cook until heated through. If soup is too thick, add additional broth, a few tablespoons at a time, until soup reaches desired consistency. Sprinkle with pumpkin seeds, if desired.

Pumpkin Mac and Cheese

Makes 6 to 8 servings

1 package (16 ounces) uncooked large elbow macaroni

½ cup (1 stick) butter, divided

¼ cup all-purpose flour

1½ cups milk

1 teaspoon salt, divided

¼ teaspoon ground nutmeg

⅛ teaspoon ground red pepper

2 cups (8 ounces) shredded Cheddar cheese

1 cup (4 ounces) shredded Monterey Jack cheese

1 cup canned pumpkin

1 cup panko bread crumbs

½ cup chopped hazelnuts or walnuts (optional)

⅛ teaspoon dried sage

1 cup (4 ounces) shredded Chihuahua cheese*

If Chihuahua cheese is not available, substitute Monterey Jack cheese.

1. Preheat oven to 350°F. Spray 2-quart baking dish with nonstick cooking spray. Cook macaroni according to package directions until al dente. Drain and return to saucepan; keep warm.

2. Melt ¼ cup butter in medium saucepan over medium-high heat. Whisk in flour until smooth; cook 1 minute without browning, whisking constantly. Gradually whisk in milk in thin, steady stream. Add ¾ teaspoon salt, nutmeg and red pepper; cook 2 to 3 minutes or until thickened, stirring frequently. Gradually add Cheddar and Monterey Jack, stirring after each addition until smooth. Add pumpkin; cook 1 minute or until heated through, stirring constantly. Pour sauce over pasta; stir to coat.

3. Melt remaining ¼ cup butter in small skillet over medium-low heat; cook until golden brown. Remove from heat; stir in panko, hazelnuts, if desired, sage and remaining ¼ teaspoon salt.

4. Spread half of pasta in prepared baking dish; sprinkle with ½ cup Chihuahua cheese. Top with remaining pasta; sprinkle with remaining Chihuahua cheese. Top with panko mixture.

5. Bake 25 to 30 minutes or until topping is golden brown and pasta is heated through.

Pumpkin Seed Spread

Makes about ¾ cup (about 6 servings)

1 cup raw pumpkin seeds

2½ tablespoons honey or
  agave syrup

½ teaspoon ground cinnamon

¼ teaspoon salt

2 to 4 tablespoons olive
  or vegetable oil

1. Preheat oven to 350°F. Spread pumpkin seeds on ungreased baking sheet. Bake 8 to 10 minutes or until golden brown, stirring occasionally. Cool completely.

2. Place pumpkin seeds in food processor; pulse until finely ground and powdery. Add honey, cinnamon and salt; pulse until combined. With motor running, slowly add oil; process 3 to 4 minutes or until smooth paste forms.

Serving Suggestion: Use this spread like peanut butter; try it with jam on crackers or toast. Or for a fun, kid-friendly snack, serve it on celery sticks with raisins.

Pumpkin Curry

Makes 4 servings

1 tablespoon vegetable oil

1 package (14 ounces) firm tofu, drained, patted dry and cut into 1-inch cubes

¼ cup Thai red curry paste

2 cloves garlic, minced

1 can (15 ounces) pure pumpkin

1 can (13 ounces) coconut milk

1 cup vegetable broth or water

1½ teaspoons salt

1 teaspoon sriracha sauce

4 cups cut-up fresh vegetables (broccoli, cauliflower, red bell pepper and/or sweet potato)

½ cup peas

Hot cooked rice

¼ cup shredded fresh basil (optional)

1. Heat oil in wok or large skillet over high heat. Add tofu; stir-fry 5 minutes or until lightly browned. Add curry paste and garlic; cook and stir 1 minute or until tofu is coated.

2. Add pumpkin, coconut milk, broth, salt and sriracha; bring to a boil. Stir in vegetables. Reduce heat to medium; cover and cook 20 minutes or until vegetables are tender.

3. Stir in peas; cook 1 minute or until heated through. Serve over rice; top with basil, if desired.

Harvest Pumpkin Soup

Makes 8 servings

◇◇◇

1   sugar pumpkin or acorn
    squash (about 2 pounds)
1   kabocha or butternut squash
    (about 2 pounds)
    Salt and black pepper
2   tablespoons olive oil
2   tablespoons butter
1   large onion, finely chopped
2   stalks celery, chopped
1   medium carrot, chopped
¼   cup packed brown sugar
2   tablespoons tomato paste
1   tablespoon minced
    fresh ginger
1   clove garlic, minced
1   teaspoon salt
1   teaspoon ground cinnamon
¼   teaspoon ground cumin
¼   teaspoon black pepper
4   cups vegetable broth
1   cup milk
2   teaspoons lemon juice
    Roasted pumpkin seeds
    (optional, see Tip)

1. Preheat oven to 400°F. Line large baking sheet with foil; spray with nonstick cooking spray.

2. Cut pumpkin and kabocha squash in half; remove and discard seeds and strings or reserve seeds to roast (see Tip). Season cut sides with salt and pepper. Place cut sides down on prepared baking sheet; bake 30 to 45 minutes or until fork-tender. When squash is cool enough to handle, remove skin; chop flesh into 1-inch pieces.

3. Heat oil and butter in large saucepan or Dutch oven over medium-high heat. Add onion, celery and carrot; cook and stir 5 minutes or until vegetables are tender. Add brown sugar, tomato paste, ginger, garlic, 1 teaspoon salt, cinnamon, cumin and ¼ teaspoon pepper; cook and stir 1 minute. Stir in broth and squash; bring to a boil. Reduce heat to medium; cook 20 minutes or until squash is very soft.

4. Process soup in batches in food processor or blender until smooth. (Or use hand-held immersion blender.) Return soup to saucepan. Stir in milk and lemon juice; cook until heated through. Garnish with pumpkin seeds.

Tip: Roasted pumpkin seeds can be found at many supermarkets, or you can roast the seeds that you remove from the pumpkin (or the squash) in the recipe. Toss the seeds with 1 teaspoon vegetable oil and ⅛ teaspoon salt in a small bowl; spread on a small foil-lined baking sheet. Bake at 300°F 20 to 25 minutes or until the seeds begin to brown, stirring once.

Baked Ravioli with Pumpkin Sauce

Makes 4 servings

1 package (9 ounces)
   refrigerated cheese ravioli

1 tablespoon butter

1 shallot, finely chopped

1 cup whipping cream

1 cup canned pumpkin

½ cup grated Asiago cheese,
   divided

½ teaspoon salt

¼ teaspoon ground nutmeg

⅛ teaspoon black pepper

½ cup coarse plain dry bread
   crumbs or small croutons

1. Preheat oven to 350°F. Spray 2-quart baking dish with nonstick cooking spray.

2. Cook ravioli according to package directions. Drain well; cover and keep warm.

3. Meanwhile, melt butter in medium saucepan over medium heat. Add shallot; cook and stir 3 minutes or until tender. Reduce heat to low. Add cream, pumpkin, ¼ cup cheese, salt, nutmeg and pepper; cook and stir 2 minutes or until cheese melts. Gently stir in ravioli.

4. Spoon ravioli mixture into prepared baking dish. Combine remaining ¼ cup cheese and bread crumbs in small bowl; sprinkle over ravioli.

5. Bake 15 minutes or until heated through and topping is lightly browned.

Pumpkin Chile Cheese Dip

Makes about 2 cups

1 tablespoon butter

¼ cup finely chopped green
   bell pepper

2 tablespoons finely chopped
   onion

1 can (10¾ ounces) condensed
   nacho cheese soup,*
   undiluted

1 cup canned pumpkin

½ cup half-and-half

1 to 2 teaspoons minced canned
   chipotle peppers in adobo
   sauce

¼ teaspoon salt

   Tortilla chips and/or
   vegetables

*If nacho cheese soup is unavailable,
substitute Cheddar cheese soup and
add additional ½ teaspoon chipotle
pepper.

1. Melt butter in medium saucepan over medium heat. Add bell pepper and onion; cook and stir 3 minutes or until vegetables are tender.

2. Reduce heat to low. Stir in soup, pumpkin, half-and-half, 1 teaspoon chipotle pepper and salt; cook 10 minutes, stirring frequently. Taste and add additional chipotle pepper, if desired. Serve warm with tortilla chips and/or vegetables for dipping.

Note: Two teaspoons of chipotle pepper will make a very spicy dip. Start with 1 teaspoon and taste before adding additional chipotle pepper.

Cakes & Cheesecakes

Pumpkin Poke Cake

Makes 12 to 16 servings

1 package (about 15 ounces)
   yellow cake mix, plus
   ingredients to prepare mix

1 can (15 ounces) pure pumpkin

1 can (14 ounces) sweetened
   condensed milk

2 teaspoons ground cinnamon

1 container (8 ounces) frozen
   whipped topping, thawed

2 cups chopped toffee bits

1 jar (12 ounces) caramel
   ice cream topping

1. Prepare and bake cake mix according to package directions for 13×9-inch pan. Cool completely in pan on wire rack.

2. Poke holes in cake at $\frac{1}{2}$-inch intervals with wooden skewer.

3. Whisk pumpkin, sweetened condensed milk and cinnamon in medium bowl until well blended. Pour over cake, spreading evenly; top with whipped topping and toffee bits. Refrigerate 2 to 3 hours or until firm.

4. Drizzle caramel topping over cake just before serving.

Pumpkin Cheesecake

Makes 12 to 14 servings

Crust

18 graham crackers (2 sleeves)

¼ cup sugar

⅛ teaspoon salt

½ cup (1 stick) butter, melted

Filling

1 can (15 ounces) pure pumpkin

¼ cup sour cream

2 teaspoons vanilla

2 teaspoons ground cinnamon, plus additional for garnish

1 teaspoon ground ginger

¼ teaspoon salt

¼ teaspoon ground cloves

4 packages (8 ounces each) cream cheese, softened

1¾ cups sugar

5 eggs

Whipped cream

1. Line bottom of 9-inch springform pan with parchment paper. Spray bottom and side of pan with nonstick cooking spray. Wrap outside of pan with heavy-duty foil.

2. For crust, place graham crackers in food processor; pulse until fine crumbs form. Add ¼ cup sugar and ⅛ teaspoon salt; pulse to blend. Add butter; pulse until crumbs are moistened and mixture is well blended. Press onto bottom and all the way up side of prepared pan in thin layer. Refrigerate at least 20 minutes. Preheat oven to 350°F.

3. Bake crust 12 minutes; cool on wire rack. Bring large pot of water to a boil.

4. For filling, whisk pumpkin, sour cream, vanilla, 2 teaspoons cinnamon, ginger, ¼ teaspoon salt and cloves in medium bowl until well blended. Beat cream cheese and 1¾ cups sugar in large bowl with electric mixer at medium speed until smooth and creamy. With mixer running, beat in eggs, one at a time, until blended. Scrape side of bowl. Add pumpkin mixture; beat at medium speed until well blended. Pour into crust. Place springform pan in large roasting pan; place in oven. Carefully add boiling water to roasting pan to come about halfway up side of springform pan.

5. Bake 1 hour 15 minutes or until top is set and lightly browned but center jiggles slightly. Remove cheesecake from water; remove foil. Cool to room temperature on wire rack.

Run small thin spatula around edge of pan to loosen crust. (Do not remove side of pan.) Cover with plastic wrap; refrigerate 8 hours or overnight. Garnish with whipped cream and additional cinnamon.

Quick Pumpkin Chocolate Chip Bundt Cake

Makes 12 servings

1 package (about 15 ounces) spice cake mix

1 can (15 ounces) pure pumpkin

2 eggs

⅓ cup water

1 cup semisweet chocolate chips

1 cup semisweet chocolate chips, melted (optional)

1. Preheat oven to 350°F. Grease and flour 12-cup (10-inch) bundt pan.

2. Combine cake mix, pumpkin, eggs and water in large bowl; beat 1 to 2 minutes or until well blended. Stir in 1 cup chocolate chips. Pour batter into prepared pan.

3. Bake 35 to 40 minutes or until toothpick inserted near center comes out clean. Cool in pan 10 minutes; invert onto wire rack to cool completely.

4. Drizzle melted chocolate over cooled cake, if desired.

Celebration Pumpkin Cake

Makes 12 servings

1 package (about 15 ounces) spice cake mix

1 can (15 ounces) pure pumpkin

3 eggs

¼ cup (½ stick) butter, softened

1½ containers (16 ounces each) cream cheese frosting

⅓ cup caramel ice cream topping

Pecan halves (optional)

1. Preheat oven to 350°F. Grease and flour three 9-inch round cake pans.

2. Beat cake mix, pumpkin, eggs and butter in large bowl with electric mixer at medium speed 2 minutes or until well blended. Pour batter into prepared pans.

3. Bake 20 minutes or until toothpick inserted into centers comes out clean. Cool in pans 15 minutes; remove to wire racks to cool completely.

4. Place one cake layer on serving plate; spread with one fourth of frosting. Repeat layers two times. Spread remaining frosting on side of cake. Spread caramel topping over top of cake, allowing some to drip down side. Garnish with pecans.

Southern Pumpkin Cheesecake

Makes 12 to 14 servings

1¾ cups graham cracker crumbs

1 cup sugar, divided

½ cup (1 stick) butter, melted

1 package (8 ounces) cream cheese, softened

2 eggs

¾ cup milk

2 packages (4-serving size each) French vanilla instant pudding and pie filling mix

2 cups canned pumpkin

⅛ teaspoon ground cinnamon

1 container (12 ounces) frozen whipped topping, thawed, divided

Dash ground nutmeg

1. Preheat oven to 350°F. Combine graham cracker crumbs, ¼ cup sugar and butter in small bowl; mix well. Press into bottom of 9-inch springform pan.

2. Beat cream cheese, eggs and remaining ¾ cup sugar in medium bowl with electric mixer at medium speed 3 minutes or until light and fluffy. Pour into crust.

3. Bake 20 minutes. Remove to wire rack to cool completely.

4. Beat milk and pudding mix in large bowl with electric mixer at medium speed 2 minutes. Add pumpkin and cinnamon; beat until well blended. Stir in 1 cup whipped topping until blended.

5. Spread pudding mixture over cream cheese layer. Pipe or spread remaining whipped topping over pudding layer. Sprinkle with nutmeg. Refrigerate 4 hours or overnight.

Pumpkin Cake with Cream Cheese Glaze

Makes 12 to 16 servings

Cake

- 2 cups all-purpose flour
- 2 teaspoons baking powder
- 2 teaspoons ground cinnamon
- 1 teaspoon baking soda
- 1 teaspoon salt
- 1 teaspoon ground ginger
- 1 teaspoon ground nutmeg
- 1 can (15 ounces) pure pumpkin
- 3 eggs
- ¾ cup packed brown sugar
- ½ cup granulated sugar
- ½ cup unsweetened applesauce
- 2 tablespoons vegetable oil

Glaze

- 2 ounces cream cheese, softened
- ¼ cup powdered sugar
- 2 to 4 tablespoons milk

1. Preheat oven to 350°F. Spray 13×9-inch baking pan with nonstick cooking spray.

2. Combine flour, baking powder, cinnamon, baking soda, salt, ginger and nutmeg in medium bowl; mix well. Whisk pumpkin, eggs, brown sugar, granulated sugar, applesauce and oil in large bowl until smooth and well blended. Gradually add flour mixture; stir until well blended. Pour batter into prepared pan.

3. Bake 30 to 35 minutes or until toothpick inserted into center comes out clean. Cool completely in pan on wire rack.

4. Beat cream cheese in medium bowl until smooth. Add powdered sugar; beat until well blended. Add 2 tablespoons milk; beat until smooth. Add additional milk, 1 teaspoon at a time, until desired consistency is reached.

5. Spread glaze over cake; let stand until set.

Pumpkin Pie Surprise Cupcakes

Makes 22 cupcakes

1 package (about 15 ounces) yellow cake mix, plus ingredients to prepare mix

1 teaspoon ground cinnamon

1 refrigerated pie crust (half of 14-ounce package)

3 cups whipping cream

1½ cups canned pumpkin pie mix

Ground nutmeg (optional)

1. Preheat oven to 350°F. Line 22 standard (2½-inch) muffin cups with paper baking cups.

2. Prepare cake mix according to package directions, stirring cinnamon into batter. Spoon batter evenly into prepared muffin cups. Bake 20 minutes or until toothpick inserted into centers comes out clean. Cool completely in pans on wire racks.

3. Meanwhile, prepare pumpkin cutouts. *Increase oven temperature to 400°F.* Line baking sheet with parchment paper. Unroll pie crust on work surface; use cookie cutter or sharp paring knife to cut out 22 small (1- to 2-inch) pumpkins. Place cutouts on prepared baking sheet; score vertical lines in each pumpkin to resemble ridges. Bake 10 minutes or until light golden brown. Remove to wire racks to cool completely.

4. Beat cream in large bowl with electric mixer at medium-high speed until stiff peaks form. Whisk 1 cup whipped cream and pumpkin pie mix in medium bowl until well blended.

5. Cut hole in top of each cupcake (about 1 inch wide and 1 inch deep); discard cupcake pieces. Fill each hole with about 1 tablespoon pumpkin filling. Pipe or spread remaining whipped cream over cupcakes. Sprinkle lightly with nutmeg, if desired. Top with pumpkin cutouts.

Sticky Caramel Pumpkin Cake

Makes 8 servings

2 cups all-purpose flour

2 teaspoons baking powder

1 teaspoon baking soda

½ teaspoon salt

½ teaspoon pumpkin pie spice
   or ground cinnamon

1⅓ cups sugar

1 cup (2 sticks) butter, softened

4 eggs, at room temperature

1 can (15 ounces) pure pumpkin

1 cup caramel sauce or caramel
   ice cream topping, divided

Slow Cooker Directions

1. Spray 4½-quart slow cooker with nonstick cooking spray.

2. Combine flour, baking powder, baking soda, salt and pumpkin pie spice in large bowl; mix well. Beat sugar and butter in another large bowl with electric mixer at high speed 3 minutes or until light. Add eggs, one at a time, beating well after each addition. Beat in pumpkin until blended. Gradually add flour mixture; beat at low speed until smooth. Spread batter evenly in slow cooker.

3. Cover; cook on HIGH 2 to 2½ hours or until toothpick inserted into center of cake comes out clean. Let cake stand, uncovered, 10 minutes. Invert onto wire rack; invert again onto serving plate. Drizzle ¼ to ⅓ cup caramel sauce over cake. Serve warm with remaining caramel sauce.

Variation: To bake this cake in a conventional oven, spray a 2- to 2½-quart round baking dish with nonstick cooking spray; line the bottom of the dish with parchment paper. Prepare the batter as directed; pour into the baking dish and smooth the top. Bake in a preheated 350°F oven 1 hour 10 minutes or until the top is golden brown and a wooden skewer inserted into the center comes out almost clean. Remove to a wire rack to cool 10 minutes. Invert the cake onto the wire rack; invert again onto a serving plate. Drizzle with ¼ to ⅓ cup caramel sauce; serve warm with the remaining sauce.

Classic Pumpkin Roll

Makes 10 servings

1 package (about 16 ounces) angel food cake mix

1¼ cups water

1¼ cups powdered sugar, divided

1 package (8 ounces) cream cheese, softened

1 container (8 ounces) whipped topping, thawed

½ cup canned pumpkin

Cream Cheese Frosting (recipe follows)

½ cup chopped hazelnuts (optional)

1. Preheat oven to 350°F. Spray 17×12-inch jelly-roll pan with nonstick cooking spray. Line pan with parchment or waxed paper.

2. Beat cake mix and water in large bowl according to package directions. Pour batter into prepared pan. Bake 17 minutes or until toothpick inserted into center comes out clean. Immediately invert cake onto clean towel sprinkled with ½ cup powdered sugar. Remove parchment paper. Starting from short side, roll up cake and towel jelly-roll style. Place seam side down on wire rack; cool completely.

3. Beat cream cheese and remaining ¾ cup powdered sugar in large bowl with electric mixer at medium speed 2 minutes or until light and fluffy. Fold in whipped topping and pumpkin until well blended. Refrigerate until ready to use. Prepare Cream Cheese Frosting.

4. Carefully unroll cake onto serving plate, removing towel. Spread pumpkin filling evenly over cake. Re-roll cake; place seam side down on plate. (If cake breaks, hold pieces together and roll as directed. Breaks can later be hidden with frosting.)

5. Frost with Cream Cheese Frosting; sprinkle with hazelnuts, if desired. Trim 1 inch off each end with serrated knife; discard scraps. Cover with plastic wrap; refrigerate 2 to 3 hours before serving.

Cream Cheese Frosting: Beat 2 packages (8 ounces each) softened cream cheese and ½ cup (1 stick) softened butter in large bowl with electric mixer at medium-high speed 3 minutes or until light and fluffy. Add 2 cups powdered sugar, sifted, and 2 teaspoons vanilla; beat until well blended.

Cranberry Swirl Pumpkin Cheesecake

Makes 8 servings

Graham Cracker Crust
  (recipe follows)

2 packages (8 ounces each)
  cream cheese, softened

¾ cup sugar

1 teaspoon vanilla

2 eggs

1 can (15 ounces) pure pumpkin

1 teaspoon ground cinnamon

½ teaspoon ground ginger

½ teaspoon ground nutmeg

½ teaspoon ground cloves

⅛ teaspoon salt

1 can (14 ounces) whole berry
  cranberry sauce

1. Preheat oven to 350°F. Prepare Graham Cracker Crust.

2. Beat cream cheese, sugar and vanilla in large bowl with electric mixer at medium speed about 3 minutes or until smooth and creamy. Add eggs, one at a time, beating well after each addition. Add pumpkin, cinnamon, ginger, nutmeg, cloves and salt; beat until well blended.

3. Spread ¾ cup batter evenly in prepared crust. Stir cranberry sauce; pour about half of sauce over batter. Top with remaining pumpkin mixture and cranberry sauce. Gently swirl cranberry sauce with tip of knife, being careful not to scrape crust.

4. Bake 1 hour. (Cheesecake will not be completely set in center.) Cool completely in pan on wire rack. Refrigerate at least 2 hours or overnight.

Graham Cracker Crust: Place 26 to 30 square graham crackers in food processor, breaking into smaller pieces if necessary. Pulse until finely crushed. (Or substitute 1½ cups prepared graham cracker crumbs.) Combine graham cracker crumbs, ⅓ cup sugar and ⅓ cup melted butter in medium bowl; mix well. Press firmly into bottom and up side of 10-inch deep-dish pie plate. Bake in preheated 350°F oven 8 minutes or until browned. Cool completely on wire rack.

Cider-Glazed Pumpkin Bundt Cakes

Makes 10 cakes

◇◇

1 package (about 15 ounces) spice cake mix

1 can (15 ounces) pure pumpkin

3 eggs

⅔ cup water

⅓ cup vegetable oil

4 cups plus 2 tablespoons apple cider, divided

16 whole cloves

½ teaspoon ground cinnamon

1½ teaspoons cornstarch

1. Preheat oven to 350°F. Grease and flour 10 mini (1-cup) bundt pan cups.

2. Combine cake mix, pumpkin, eggs, water and oil in large bowl; beat until well blended. Spoon batter evenly into prepared bundt pan cups (about ½ cup batter per cup).

3. Bake 30 minutes or until toothpick inserted near centers comes out clean. Cool in pans 15 minutes; invert onto wire racks to cool completely.

4. Meanwhile, combine 4 cups cider, cloves and cinnamon in nonstick skillet; bring to a boil over high heat. Boil 7 minutes or until liquid has reduced to 1 cup. Whisk cornstarch into remaining 2 tablespoons cider in small bowl until smooth. Add to cider mixture; cook and stir until slightly thickened. Remove from heat; cool completely.

5. Remove and discard cloves. Spoon glaze over cakes.

Pumpkin Pecan Dump Cake

Makes 12 to 16 servings

1 can (15 ounces) pure pumpkin

1 can (12 ounces) evaporated milk

1 cup packed brown sugar

3 eggs

2 teaspoons pumpkin pie spice

½ teaspoon salt

1 package (about 15 ounces) yellow cake mix

¾ cup (1½ sticks) butter, cut into thin slices

½ cup pecan halves

1. Preheat oven to 350°F. Spray 13×9-inch baking pan with nonstick cooking spray.

2. Whisk pumpkin, evaporated milk, brown sugar, eggs, pumpkin pie spice and salt in medium bowl until well blended. Pour into prepared pan. Spread dry cake mix evenly over pumpkin mixture.

3. Top with butter in single layer, covering cake mix as much as possible. Sprinkle with pecans.

4. Bake about 1 hour or until toothpick inserted into center of cake comes out clean. Cool completely in pan on wire rack.

Marbled Pumpkin Cheesecake

Makes 14 to 16 servings

Gingersnap Cookie Crust
(recipe follows)

4 packages (8 ounces each)
cream cheese, softened

½ cup sugar

6 eggs

1 cup sour cream

1 cup canned pumpkin

2 tablespoons all-purpose flour

2 teaspoons ground cinnamon

½ teaspoon ground ginger

½ teaspoon ground allspice

3 ounces semisweet chocolate,
melted

1. Prepare Gingersnap Cookie Crust.

2. *Increase oven temperature to 425°F.* Beat cream cheese in large bowl with electric mixer at medium-high speed about 3 minutes or until light and fluffy. Add sugar; beat until well blended. Add eggs, one at a time, beating well after each addition. Add sour cream, pumpkin, flour, cinnamon, ginger and allspice; beat until well blended.

3. Pour 2 cups batter into small bowl; stir in melted chocolate until well blended. Pour remaining batter into prepared crust. Spoon chocolate batter in large swirls over pumpkin batter in crust; draw knife through mixture to marbleize.

4. Bake 15 minutes. *Reduce oven temperature to 300°F.* Bake 45 minutes (center of cheesecake will not be set). Turn off oven; let cheesecake stand in oven with door slightly ajar 1 hour. Cool to room temperature in pan on wire rack. Cover and refrigerate overnight.

Gingersnap Cookie Crust: Preheat oven to 350°F. Combine 1 cup gingersnap cookie crumbs, ½ cup graham cracker crumbs and ¼ cup sugar in small bowl; mix well. Stir in 5 tablespoons melted butter until well blended. Press into bottom and 1 inch up side of 9-inch springform pan. Bake 8 minutes. Cool completely on wire rack.

Pumpkin Spice Cake

Makes 12 to 16 servings

1¾ cups all-purpose flour

¾ cup packed brown sugar

2 teaspoons ground cinnamon

1¾ teaspoons baking powder

1 teaspoon baking soda

1 teaspoon salt

1 teaspoon ground ginger

¼ teaspoon ground nutmeg

¼ teaspoon ground cloves

1 can (15 ounces) pure pumpkin

4 eggs

⅔ cup vegetable or canola oil

1 cup raisins

Powdered sugar (optional)

1. Preheat oven to 350°F. Spray 13×9-inch pan with nonstick cooking spray.

2. Combine flour, brown sugar, cinnamon, baking powder, baking soda, salt, ginger, nutmeg and cloves in large bowl; mix well. Add pumpkin, eggs and oil; beat with electric mixer at medium speed 1 minute or until well blended. Stir in raisins. Pour batter into prepared pan.

3. Bake about 30 minutes or until toothpick inserted into center comes out clean. Cool completely in pan on wire rack. Sprinkle with powdered sugar just before serving, if desired.

Pumpkin Cheesecake with Gingersnap-Pecan Crust

Makes 10 to 12 servings

1¼ cups gingersnap cookie crumbs (about 24 cookies)

⅓ cup pecans, very finely chopped, plus additional for garnish

¼ cup granulated sugar

¼ cup (½ stick) butter, melted

3 packages (8 ounces each) cream cheese, softened

1 cup packed brown sugar

1 teaspoon ground cinnamon

½ teaspoon ground ginger

¼ teaspoon ground nutmeg

2 eggs

2 egg yolks

1 cup canned pumpkin

Whipped cream (optional)

1. Preheat oven to 350°F. Combine cookie crumbs, ⅓ cup pecans, granulated sugar and butter in medium bowl; mix well. Press mixture evenly into bottom of ungreased 9-inch springform pan. Bake 8 to 10 minutes or until golden brown. Cool completely on wire rack.

2. Meanwhile, beat cream cheese in large bowl with electric mixer at medium speed about 3 minutes or until fluffy. Add brown sugar, cinnamon, ginger and nutmeg; beat until well blended. Add eggs and egg yolks, one at a time, beating well after each addition. Beat in pumpkin until blended. Pour batter over crust.

3. Bake 1 hour or until edge is set but center is still moist. Turn off oven; let cheesecake stand in oven with door slightly ajar 30 minutes. Remove to wire rack. Loosen edge of cheesecake from side of pan with thin metal spatula; cool completely in pan on wire rack.

4. Cover and refrigerate at least 24 hours or up to 48 hours before serving. Top with whipped cream and additional pecans, if desired.

Tip: If your springform pan doesn't seal tightly, wrap the bottom of the pan with foil to prevent butter from leaking out of the crust during baking.

Cinnamon Pecan Pumpkin Cake

Makes 12 to 16 servings

2 cups all-purpose flour

1 cup granulated sugar

¾ cup packed dark brown sugar

2 teaspoons baking powder

2 teaspoons pumpkin pie spice

1 teaspoon salt

1 can (15 ounces) pure pumpkin

½ cup vegetable oil

½ cup milk

2 eggs

1 teaspoon vanilla

¾ cup cinnamon chips, divided

½ cup chopped pecans, divided

1. Preheat oven to 350°F. Grease 13×9-inch baking pan or line with parchment paper.

2. Combine flour, granulated sugar, brown sugar, baking powder, pumpkin pie spice and salt in large bowl; mix well. Whisk pumpkin, oil, milk, eggs and vanilla in medium bowl until blended. Add to flour mixture; stir just until blended. Stir in ½ cup cinnamon chips and ¼ cup pecans. Spread batter in prepared pan; sprinkle with remaining cinnamon chips and pecans.

3. Bake 25 to 30 minutes or until toothpick inserted into center comes out clean. Cool in pan at least 15 minutes before serving.

Pumpkin Spice Mug Cake

Makes 1 serving

¼ cup angel food cake mix

3 tablespoons water

2 teaspoons canned pumpkin

1 teaspoon finely chopped pecans

¼ teaspoon pumpkin pie spice

Whipped topping (optional)

Ground cinnamon and sugar (optional)

Microwave Directions

1. Combine cake mix, water, pumpkin, pecans and pumpkin pie spice in large ceramic* microwavable mug; mix well.

2. Microwave on HIGH 2 minutes. Let stand 1 to 2 minutes before serving. Garnish with whipped topping; sprinkle with cinnamon and sugar, if desired.

*This cake requires a ceramic mug, as the material allows for more even cooking than glass.

Pies & Tarts

Spiced Pumpkin Pie
Makes 8 servings

Pie dough for single-crust
   9-inch pie

1 can (15 ounces) pure pumpkin

¾ cup packed brown sugar

2 teaspoons ground cinnamon

¾ teaspoon ground ginger

½ teaspoon ground nutmeg,
   plus additional for garnish

¼ teaspoon salt

⅛ teaspoon ground cloves

4 eggs, lightly beaten

1 cup light cream or
   half-and-half

1 teaspoon vanilla

Optional garnishes:
   dried cranberries, pumpkin
   seeds and pecan halves

1. Preheat oven to 400°F. Line 9-inch pie plate with dough; trim edge even with edge of pie plate or flute edge.

2. Whisk pumpkin, brown sugar, cinnamon, ginger, ½ teaspoon nutmeg, salt and cloves in large bowl until well blended. Add eggs; whisk until blended. Gradually whisk in cream and vanilla until well blended. Pour into unbaked crust.

3. Bake 40 to 45 minutes or until knife inserted near center comes out clean. Cool completely on wire rack. Serve warm or at room temperature; garnish as desired.

Praline Pumpkin Tart

Makes 8 servings

1¼ cups all-purpose flour

1 tablespoon granulated sugar

¾ teaspoon salt, divided

¼ cup cold shortening,
   cut into small pieces

¼ cup (½ stick) cold butter,
   cut into small pieces

3 to 4 tablespoons cold water

1 can (15 ounces) pure pumpkin

1 can (12 ounces) evaporated
   milk

⅔ cup packed brown sugar

2 eggs

1 teaspoon ground cinnamon

½ teaspoon ground ginger

¼ teaspoon ground cloves

Praline Topping
   (recipe follows)

1. Combine flour, granulated sugar and ¼ teaspoon salt in large bowl; mix well. Cut in shortening and butter with pastry blender or two knives until coarse crumbs form.

2. Sprinkle flour mixture with water, 1 tablespoon at a time. Toss with fork until mixture holds together. Shape dough into a ball; wrap with plastic wrap. Refrigerate about 1 hour or until chilled.

3. Roll out dough into 13×9-inch rectangle on lightly floured surface. Press into bottom and up sides of 11×7-inch baking dish. Cover with plastic wrap; refrigerate 30 minutes.

4. Preheat oven to 400°F. Prick bottom of crust all over with fork. Top with foil; fill crust with dried beans, uncooked rice or ceramic pie weights. Bake 10 minutes or until set.

5. Remove from oven; gently remove foil lining and beans. Return crust to oven; bake 5 minutes or until golden brown. Cool completely on wire rack.

6. Whisk pumpkin, evaporated milk, brown sugar, eggs, cinnamon, remaining ½ teaspoon salt, ginger and cloves in large bowl until well blended. Pour into prepared crust. Bake 35 minutes.

7. Meanwhile, prepare Praline Topping. Sprinkle topping over tart. Bake 15 minutes or until knife inserted 1 inch from center comes out clean. Cool completely on wire rack.

Praline Topping: Combine ⅓ cup packed brown sugar, ⅓ cup chopped pecans and ⅓ cup quick oats in small bowl. Cut in 1 tablespoon butter with pastry blender or two knives until coarse crumbs form.

Maple Pumpkin Pie

Makes 8 servings

1 refrigerated deep-dish
   pie crust

1 can (15 ounces) pure pumpkin

1 can (12 ounces) evaporated
   milk

2 eggs

⅓ cup sugar

⅓ cup maple syrup, plus
   additional for garnish

1 teaspoon ground cinnamon,
   plus additional for garnish

½ teaspoon ground ginger

½ teaspoon salt

   Whipped cream (optional)

1. Preheat oven to 425°F. Press crust into 9-inch deep-dish pie plate; flute edge as desired.

2. Whisk pumpkin, evaporated milk, eggs, sugar, ⅓ cup maple syrup, 1 teaspoon cinnamon, ginger and salt in large bowl until well blended. Pour into unbaked crust.

3. Bake 15 minutes. *Reduce oven temperature to 350°F.* Bake 40 minutes or until center is set. Remove to wire rack to cool at least 30 minutes before serving.

4. Serve pie warm, at room temperature or chilled. Garnish with whipped cream, additional maple syrup and cinnamon.

Crustless Pumpkin Pie

Makes 4 servings

¼ cup coarsely crushed cornflakes

¼ cup plus 1 tablespoon packed brown sugar, divided

1 teaspoon ground cinnamon, divided

¼ teaspoon plus ⅛ teaspoon ground ginger, divided

¾ cup evaporated milk

1 teaspoon cornstarch

¼ teaspoon ground nutmeg

¾ cup canned pumpkin

2 tablespoons corn syrup

1 egg, beaten

1. Preheat oven to 350°F. Combine cornflakes, 1 tablespoon brown sugar, ½ teaspoon cinnamon and ⅛ teaspoon ginger in medium bowl; mix well.

2. Heat evaporated milk in small saucepan over medium heat. *Do not boil.* Combine remaining ¼ cup brown sugar, ½ teaspoon cinnamon, ¼ teaspoon ginger, cornstarch and nutmeg in small bowl; mix well.

3. Place pumpkin in large bowl; whisk in brown sugar mixture and corn syrup until well blended. Gradually add hot milk; whisk until well blended. Add egg; whisk until smooth. Pour into four 6-ounce custard cups or ramekins.

4. Place cups in baking pan; add hot water to baking pan to depth of ¾ inch. Sprinkle cornflake topping over custard.

5. Bake 35 to 40 minutes or until knife inserted into center of custard comes out clean.

Pumpkin Pecan Pie

Makes 8 to 10 servings

◇◇◇◇◇◇◇◇◇◇◇◇◇◇◇◇◇◇◇◇◇◇◇◇◇◇◇◇◇◇◇◇◇◇◇

1 can (15 ounces) pure pumpkin

1 can (14 ounces) sweetened
   condensed milk

¼ cup (½ stick) butter, softened

2 eggs, divided

1 teaspoon ground cinnamon

1 teaspoon vanilla

½ teaspoon ground nutmeg,
   plus additional for serving

¼ teaspoon salt

1 (6-ounce) graham cracker
   pie crust

2 tablespoons packed
   brown sugar

2 tablespoons dark corn syrup

1 tablespoon butter, melted

½ teaspoon maple flavoring

1 cup chopped pecans

Whipped cream (optional)

1. Preheat oven to 400°F.

2. Whisk pumpkin, sweetened condensed milk, ¼ cup softened butter, 1 egg, cinnamon, vanilla, ½ teaspoon nutmeg and salt in large bowl until well blended. Pour into crust.

3. Bake 20 minutes. Meanwhile, beat remaining egg, brown sugar, corn syrup, 1 tablespoon melted butter and maple flavoring in medium bowl with electric mixer at medium speed until well blended. Stir in pecans.

4. Remove pie from oven; top with pecan mixture. *Reduce oven temperature to 350°F.*

5. Bake 25 minutes or until knife inserted near center comes out clean. Cool completely on wire rack. Top with whipped cream and additional nutmeg, if desired.

Pumpkin Tartlets

Makes 12 servings

1 refrigerated pie crust
   (half of 14-ounce package)

1 can (15 ounces) pure pumpkin

¼ cup milk

1 egg

6 tablespoons sugar

¾ teaspoon ground cinnamon,
   plus additional for topping

½ teaspoon vanilla

⅛ teaspoon salt

⅛ teaspoon ground nutmeg,
   plus additional for topping

Dash ground allspice

1½ cups whipped topping

1. Preheat oven to 425°F. Spray 12 standard (2½-inch) muffin cups with nonstick cooking spray.

2. Unroll pie crust on clean work surface. Cut out 12 circles with 2½-inch biscuit cutter; discard scraps. Press one circle into each prepared muffin cup.

3. Whisk pumpkin, milk, egg, sugar, ¾ teaspoon cinnamon, vanilla, salt, ⅛ teaspoon nutmeg and allspice in medium bowl until well blended. Spoon about 2 tablespoons pumpkin mixture into each tartlet shell.

4. Bake 10 minutes. *Reduce oven temperature to 325°F.* Bake 12 to 15 minutes or until knife inserted into centers comes out clean. Remove to wire rack to cool completely.

5. Spoon 2 tablespoons whipped topping on each tartlet just before serving. Sprinkle with additional cinnamon and/or nutmeg, if desired.

Pumpkin-Sweet Potato Pie

Makes 8 servings

1 refrigerated pie crust
(half of 14-ounce package)

2 cups lightly mashed cooked
sweet potatoes*

1 can (15 ounces) pure pumpkin

1 can (14 ounces) sweetened
condensed milk

3 eggs

¼ cup (½ stick) butter,
cut into small pieces

2 teaspoons Chinese five-spice
powder

1½ teaspoons grated lemon peel

Whipped cream (optional)

*Or substitute mashed canned
sweet potatoes.*

1. Preheat oven to 350°F. Let crust stand at room temperature 15 minutes. Line 10-inch deep-dish pie plate with crust.

2. Combine sweet potatoes, pumpkin, sweetened condensed milk, eggs, butter, five-spice powder and lemon peel in food processor; process until smooth. Pour into crust. Place pie plate on baking sheet.

3. Bake about 55 minutes or until puffed and knife inserted 1 inch from center comes out clean. Serve warm or at room temperature with whipped cream, if desired.

Tip: For a decorative edge, cut out shapes from an additional refrigerated pie crust. Brush the edge of the pie crust lightly with water, then gently press the cutouts onto the crust. If the edge browns too quickly during baking, cover with a strip of foil.

Ginger-Spiced Pumpkin Pie

Makes 8 servings

1 cup finely crushed gingersnap cookies

¼ cup (½ stick) butter, melted

2 egg whites

¾ cup packed brown sugar

1 can (15 ounces) pure pumpkin

1 cup evaporated milk

1 teaspoon vanilla

1 teaspoon ground ginger

1 teaspoon ground cinnamon

½ teaspoon salt

Additional gingersnap cookies (optional)

1. Combine crushed cookies and butter in medium bowl; mix well. Press into bottom and up side of 9-inch pie plate. Refrigerate 30 minutes.

2. Preheat oven to 350°F. Whisk egg whites and brown sugar in large bowl until well blended. Add pumpkin, evaporated milk, vanilla, ginger, cinnamon and salt; whisk until blended. Pour into crust.

3. Bake 60 to 70 minutes or until center is set. Remove to wire rack to cool 30 minutes. Serve warm or at room temperature. Garnish with additional cookies.

Hidden Pumpkin Pies

Makes 6 servings

1½ cups canned pumpkin

1 cup evaporated milk

2 eggs

¼ cup sugar

1¼ teaspoons vanilla, divided

1 teaspoon pumpkin pie spice*

3 egg whites

¼ teaspoon cream of tartar

⅓ cup honey

Or substitute ½ teaspoon ground cinnamon, ¼ teaspoon ground ginger and ⅛ teaspoon each ground allspice and ground nutmeg.

1. Preheat oven to 350°F.

2. Whisk pumpkin, evaporated milk, eggs, sugar, 1 teaspoon vanilla and pumpkin pie spice in large bowl until well blended. Pour into six 6-ounce ramekins or custard cups.

3. Place ramekins in shallow baking pan. Add boiling water to baking pan to depth of 1 inch.

4. Bake 25 minutes or until set.

5. Meanwhile, beat egg whites, cream of tartar and remaining ¼ teaspoon vanilla in medium bowl with electric mixer at high speed until soft peaks form. Gradually add honey, beating until stiff peaks form.

6. Spread egg white mixture over tops of hot pumpkin pies. Bake 8 to 12 minutes or until tops of pies are golden brown. Let stand 10 minutes. Serve warm.

Pecan-Quinoa Crusted Pumpkin Pie

Makes 8 servings

1 package (4 ounces)
    chopped pecans

⅓ cup uncooked quinoa,
    preferably tri-colored

¼ cup packed dark brown sugar

¼ teaspoon salt

3 eggs, divided

1 can (30 ounces)
    pumpkin pie mix

1 can (5 ounces)
    evaporated milk

1 cup whipped topping
    (optional)

⅛ teaspoon ground cinnamon
    (optional)

1. Preheat oven to 350°F. Spray 9-inch deep dish pie plate with nonstick cooking spray.

2. Combine pecans, quinoa, brown sugar and salt in food processor; pulse about 2 minutes or until mixture is finely ground, scraping down side of bowl occasionally. Add 1 egg; pulse until blended. Transfer mixture to prepared pie plate; use back of spoon or fork to gently spread mixture over bottom and 1 inch up side in even layer.

3. Bake 18 to 20 minutes or until crust is slightly firm to touch and edge is light golden brown.

4. Meanwhile, combine pumpkin pie mix, evaporated milk and remaining 2 eggs in food processor; process until smooth. Pour into crust. Place pie plate on baking sheet.

5. Bake 1 hour 15 minutes or until knife inserted near center comes out clean. Cool to room temperature on wire rack; cover and refrigerate overnight to allow flavors to blend and quinoa to soften slightly. Garnish with whipped topping and cinnamon.

Tip: There's no need to clean the food processor before adding the ingredients for the pumpkin filling.

Pumpkin Tart with Maple Crème

Makes 8 servings

◇◇

1¼ cups all-purpose flour

1 tablespoon granulated sugar

¼ teaspoon salt

⅓ cup cold butter,
    cut into small pieces

3 to 4 tablespoons cold water

1 can (15 ounces) pure pumpkin

2 eggs

½ cup maple syrup

⅓ cup packed brown sugar

¼ cup whipping cream

1 teaspoon vanilla

1 teaspoon ground cinnamon

½ teaspoon ground ginger

⅛ teaspoon ground nutmeg

    Maple Crème (recipe follows)

1. Combine flour, granulated sugar and salt in medium bowl; mix well. Cut in butter with pastry blender or two knives until mixture resembles coarse crumbs. Stir in water with fork, 1 tablespoon at a time, until dough forms a ball. Wrap dough with plastic wrap; refrigerate 30 minutes.

2. Roll out dough into 12-inch circle on lightly floured surface with lightly floured rolling pin. Press dough into bottom and up side of 10-inch tart pan with removable bottom. Trim excess dough from edge of pan. Preheat oven to 400°F.

3. Whisk pumpkin, eggs, maple syrup, brown sugar, cream, vanilla, cinnamon, ginger and nutmeg in large bowl until well blended. Pour into unbaked crust.

4. Bake 20 minutes. *Reduce oven temperature to 350°F.* Bake 30 to 35 minutes or until filling is set. Cool completely on wire rack.

5. Prepare Maple Crème; serve with tart.

Maple Crème: Beat ½ cup whipping cream in large bowl with electric mixer at high speed until soft peaks form. Add 1½ tablespoons maple syrup; beat at low speed until blended. Add ¼ cup crème fraîche or sour cream; beat until well blended. Cover with plastic wrap; refrigerate until chilled.

Vanilla Pumpkin Pie

Makes 8 servings

1 package (4-serving size) vanilla instant pudding and pie filling mix

1½ cups milk

1 cup canned pumpkin

1 teaspoon sugar

¼ teaspoon ground cinnamon

¼ teaspoon ground nutmeg

1 baked 9-inch pie crust

1. Whisk pudding mix and milk in medium bowl until blended. Add pumpkin, sugar, cinnamon and nutmeg; whisk until well blended.

2. Pour filling into crust. Refrigerate 3 hours or until firm.

Tip: This pie can be made 1 day in advance and refrigerated overnight.

Pressure Cooker Pumpkin Pie

Makes 8 servings

1½ cups graham cracker crumbs

2 tablespoons granulated sugar

¼ cup (½ stick) butter, melted

1 can (15 ounces) pure pumpkin

½ cup evaporated milk

2 eggs

½ cup packed brown sugar

2 teaspoons pumpkin pie spice

1 teaspoon vanilla

½ teaspoon salt

1 cup water

Whipped cream (optional)

1. Spray 7-inch springform pan with nonstick cooking spray. Combine graham cracker crumbs and granulated sugar in small bowl; mix well. Stir in butter until well blended. Use bottom of glass or measuring cup to press mixture evenly into bottom and 1 inch up side of prepared pan. Freeze crust 10 minutes while preparing filling.

2. Whisk pumpkin, evaporated milk, eggs, brown sugar, pumpkin pie spice, vanilla and salt in medium bowl until smooth and well blended. Wrap bottom of springform pan with foil. Pour filling into crust. Cover pan with foil.

3. Pour water into pressure cooker pot; place rack in pot. Place springform pan on rack. Secure lid and move pressure release valve to sealing or locked position. Cook at high pressure 40 minutes.

4. When cooking is complete, use natural release for 10 minutes, then release remaining pressure.

5. Remove pan from pot. Uncover; cool on wire rack 1 hour. Refrigerate overnight before sliding knife around edge and removing side of pan. Serve pie with whipped cream, if desired.

Cookies & Bars

Pumpkin Streusel Bars

Makes 2 to 3 dozen bars

1½ cups all-purpose flour, divided

½ cup packed brown sugar

¼ cup (½ stick) butter,
    cut into small pieces

1 cup coarsely chopped pecans

1½ teaspoons baking powder

1 teaspoon ground cinnamon

¼ teaspoon salt

¼ teaspoon baking soda

⅛ teaspoon ground ginger

1 cup granulated sugar

1 cup canned pumpkin

½ cup vegetable oil

2 eggs

2 tablespoons butter, melted

1. Preheat oven to 350°F. Spray 13×9-inch baking pan with nonstick cooking spray or line with foil.

2. For streusel, combine ½ cup flour and brown sugar in medium bowl; mix well. Cut in ¼ cup butter with pastry blender or two knives until mixture resembles coarse crumbs. Stir in pecans.

3. Combine remaining 1 cup flour, baking powder, cinnamon, salt, baking soda and ginger in medium bowl; mix well. Beat granulated sugar, pumpkin, oil, eggs and 2 tablespoons melted butter in large bowl with electric mixer at medium speed until well blended. Gradually add flour mixture; beat until blended. Spread batter in prepared pan; sprinkle with streusel.

4. Bake 35 minutes or until toothpick inserted into center comes out clean. Cool completely in pan on wire rack.

Maple Pumpkin Gingerbread Cookies

Makes 3 dozen cookies

3⅓ cups all-purpose flour

1½ teaspoons ground ginger

1 teaspoon baking soda

½ teaspoon salt

½ teaspoon ground cinnamon

½ teaspoon ground cloves

¼ teaspoon ground nutmeg

¼ teaspoon ground black pepper

¼ cup (½ stick) butter, softened

¼ cup packed brown sugar

1 egg

½ cup plus 1½ tablespoons maple syrup, divided

½ cup canned pumpkin

¼ cup water

2 tablespoons molasses

3 ounces cream cheese, softened

¾ cup powdered sugar

1 to 2 teaspoons milk

1. Sift flour, ginger, baking soda, salt, cinnamon, cloves, nutmeg and pepper into medium bowl. Beat butter and brown sugar in large bowl with electric mixer at medium speed about 3 minutes or until light and fluffy. Beat in egg until blended. Add ½ cup maple syrup, pumpkin, water and molasses; beat until well blended.

2. Add flour mixture; beat at low speed just until blended. Shape dough into two discs; wrap with plastic wrap. Refrigerate at least 4 hours or overnight.

3. Preheat oven to 350°F. Line cookie sheets with parchment paper. Roll out half of dough to ¼-inch thickness on lightly floured surface. Cut out dough with 3-inch round cookie cutter. Place 1 inch apart on prepared cookie sheets. Repeat with remaining dough. Reroll scraps once.

4. Bake 15 to 17 minutes or until edges are lightly browned. Cool on cookie sheets 5 minutes; remove to wire racks to cool completely.

5. For icing, place cream cheese in food processor; process until smooth. Add powdered sugar and remaining 1½ tablespoons maple syrup; process until smooth. Add enough milk to reach spreadable consistency. Transfer icing to small resealable food storage bag; cut off small corner of bag. Pipe icing on cookies.

Pumpkin Biscotti

Makes about 28 biscotti

5 cups all-purpose flour

1 tablespoon baking powder

1½ teaspoons salt

1 teaspoon ground cinnamon

½ teaspoon ground ginger

Dash ground cloves

1¼ cups plus 2 tablespoons sugar

1 cup (2 sticks) butter, softened

½ (15-ounce) can pure pumpkin

2 tablespoons water

1 cup dried cranberries

½ cup chopped pistachio nuts (optional)

½ cup prepared cream cheese frosting

1. Preheat oven to 375°F. Line cookie sheets with parchment paper.

2. Combine flour, baking powder, salt, cinnamon, ginger and cloves in medium bowl; mix well. Beat sugar and butter in large bowl with electric mixer at medium speed about 3 minutes or until light and fluffy. Add pumpkin and water; beat until well blended. Gradually add flour mixture; beat at low speed until blended. Stir in cranberries and pistachios, if desired.

3. Shape dough into two logs, each about 14 inches long and 4 to 5 inches wide, on prepared cookie sheets.

4. Bake about 40 minutes or until firm to the touch. Remove from oven; cool 20 minutes. Transfer logs to cutting board; cut into 1-inch-thick slices. Arrange slices cut sides up on cookie sheets.

5. Bake 20 minutes or until dry and lightly browned. Remove to wire racks to cool completely.

6. Heat frosting in small microwavable bowl on HIGH 30 seconds or until melted. Drizzle over biscotti.

Pumpkin Cheesecake Bars

Makes about 2 dozen squares

◇◇◇◇◇◇◇◇◇◇◇◇◇◇◇◇◇◇◇◇◇◇◇◇◇◇◇◇◇◇◇◇◇◇◇◇◇◇

1½ cups gingersnap crumbs,
     plus additional for garnish

6 tablespoons (¾ stick) butter,
    melted

2 eggs

¼ cup plus 2 tablespoons sugar,
    divided

2½ teaspoons vanilla, divided

11 ounces cream cheese,
     softened

1¼ cups canned pumpkin

1 teaspoon ground cinnamon

¼ teaspoon ground ginger

¼ teaspoon ground nutmeg

¼ teaspoon ground cloves

1 cup sour cream

1. Preheat oven to 325°F. Spray 13×9-inch baking pan with nonstick cooking spray.

2. Combine 1½ cups gingersnap crumbs and butter in small bowl; mix well. Press into bottom of prepared pan. Bake 10 minutes.

3. Meanwhile, combine eggs, ¼ cup sugar and 1½ teaspoons vanilla in food processor or blender; process 1 minute or until blended. Add cream cheese and pumpkin; process until well blended and smooth. Stir in cinnamon, ginger, nutmeg and cloves. Pour evenly over hot crust.

4. Bake 40 minutes. Whisk sour cream, remaining 2 tablespoons sugar and 1 teaspoon vanilla in small bowl until blended. Remove pan from oven; spread sour cream mixture evenly over top. Bake 5 minutes. Turn off oven; open door halfway and let bars cool completely in oven.

5. Refrigerate at least 2 hours before serving. Garnish with additional gingersnap crumbs.

Harvest Pumpkin Cookies

Makes about 3 dozen cookies

2 cups all-purpose flour

1 teaspoon baking powder

1 teaspoon ground cinnamon

½ teaspoon baking soda

½ teaspoon salt

½ teaspoon ground allspice

1 cup (2 sticks) butter, softened

1 cup sugar

1 cup canned pumpkin

1 egg

1 teaspoon vanilla

1 cup chopped pecans

1 cup dried cranberries
  or raisins (optional)

Pecan halves (about 36)

1. Preheat oven to 375°F. Combine flour, baking powder, cinnamon, baking soda, salt and allspice in medium bowl; mix well.

2. Beat butter and sugar in large bowl with electric mixer at medium speed about 3 minutes or until light and fluffy. Beat in pumpkin, egg and vanilla until well blended. Gradually add flour mixture; beat at low speed just until blended. Stir in chopped pecans and cranberries, if desired.

3. Drop dough by heaping tablespoonfuls 2 inches apart onto ungreased cookie sheets; flatten slightly with back of spoon. Press one pecan half into center of each cookie.

4. Bake 10 to 12 minutes or until golden brown. Cool on cookie sheets 1 minute; remove to wire racks to cool completely.

Pumpkin Whoopie Minis

Makes about 2½ dozen sandwich cookies

1¾ cups all-purpose flour

2 teaspoons pumpkin pie spice

1 teaspoon baking powder

1 teaspoon baking soda

1 teaspoon salt, divided

1 cup packed brown sugar

½ cup (1 stick) butter, softened, divided

1 cup canned pumpkin

2 eggs, lightly beaten

¼ cup vegetable oil

1 teaspoon vanilla, divided

4 ounces cream cheese, softened

1½ cups powdered sugar

1. Preheat oven to 350°F. Line cookie sheets with parchment paper.

2. Combine flour, pumpkin pie spice, baking powder, baking soda and ¾ teaspoon salt in medium bowl; mix well. Beat brown sugar and ¼ cup butter in large bowl with electric mixer at medium speed about 2 minutes or until creamy. Beat in pumpkin, eggs, oil and ½ teaspoon vanilla until well blended. Beat in flour mixture at low speed just until blended. Drop dough by teaspoonfuls 2 inches apart onto prepared cookie sheets.

3. Bake 10 to 12 minutes or until tops spring back when lightly touched. Cool on cookie sheets 5 minutes; remove to wire racks to cool completely.

4. Meanwhile, prepare filling. Beat cream cheese and remaining ¼ cup butter in medium bowl with electric mixer at medium speed about 2 minutes or until smooth and creamy. Beat in remaining ½ teaspoon vanilla and ¼ teaspoon salt until blended. Gradually add powdered sugar; beat until light and fluffy.

5. Pipe or spread heaping teaspoon filling on flat side of half of cookies; top with remaining cookies. Store cookies in airtight container in refrigerator.

Chocolate-Dipped Pumpkin Spice Cereal Treats

Makes 2 to 3 dozen bars

¼ cup (½ stick) butter

¼ cup canned pumpkin

¼ teaspoon salt

¼ teaspoon pumpkin pie spice

¼ teaspoon vanilla

1 package (10 ounces) marshmallows

6 cups crisp rice cereal

8 ounces bittersweet or semisweet chocolate, chopped

Small nonpareils or sprinkles (optional)

1. Spray 13×9-inch baking pan with nonstick cooking spray.

2. Heat butter in large saucepan over medium heat 3 to 4 minutes or until lightly browned, stirring frequently. (Watch butter carefully to prevent burning.) Remove to small bowl.

3. Add pumpkin to saucepan; cook 1 minute, stirring constantly. Return butter to saucepan with salt, pumpkin pie spice and vanilla; stir until blended. Add marshmallows; cook and stir over low heat until mixture is melted and smooth.

4. Remove from heat; stir in cereal until well blended. Use waxed paper or greased spatula to press mixture into prepared pan. Set aside to cool completely or refrigerate 30 minutes.

5. Melt chocolate in small saucepan over low heat or in microwave oven. Cut treats into 2×1-inch rectangles or desired size bars. Dip one end of each bar into melted chocolate; place on parchment paper. Sprinkle with nonpareils, if desired. Let stand until set.

Pumpkin White Chocolate Drops

Makes about 3 dozen cookies

1 cup granulated sugar

1 cup (2 sticks) butter, softened

½ (15-ounce) can pure pumpkin

1 egg

2 cups all-purpose flour

1 teaspoon pumpkin pie spice*

½ teaspoon baking powder

¼ teaspoon baking soda

1 cup white chocolate chips

1 cup prepared cream cheese frosting

Or substitute ½ teaspoon ground cinnamon, ¼ teaspoon ground ginger and ⅛ teaspoon each ground allspice and ground nutmeg.

1. Preheat oven to 375°F. Line cookie sheets with parchment paper or spray with nonstick cooking spray.

2. Beat granulated sugar and butter in large bowl with electric mixer at medium speed about 3 minutes or until light and fluffy. Add pumpkin and egg; beat until well blended. Add flour, pumpkin pie spice, baking powder and baking soda; beat just until blended. Stir in white chocolate chips. Drop dough by tablespoonfuls about 2 inches apart onto prepared cookie sheets.

3. Bake 16 minutes or until set and lightly browned. Cool on cookie sheets 1 minute; remove to wire racks to cool completely.

4. Spread frosting over cookies.

Whole Wheat Pumpkin Bars

Makes 2 to 3 dozen bars

1 cup all-purpose flour

1 cup whole wheat flour

¾ cup sugar

1½ teaspoons baking powder

1½ teaspoons ground cinnamon

1 teaspoon baking soda

¾ teaspoon salt

½ teaspoon ground ginger

½ teaspoon ground nutmeg

1 can (15 ounces) pure pumpkin

¾ cup canola oil

2 eggs

2 tablespoons molasses

Cream Cheese Frosting (recipe follows)

½ cup mini semisweet chocolate chips (optional)

1. Preheat oven to 350°F. Spray 13×9-inch baking pan with nonstick cooking spray.

2. Combine all-purpose flour, whole wheat flour, sugar, baking powder, cinnamon, baking soda, salt, ginger and nutmeg in medium bowl; mix well. Whisk pumpkin, oil, eggs and molasses in large bowl until well blended. Add flour mixture; stir until blended. Spread batter in prepared pan. (Batter will be very thick.)

3. Bake 20 to 25 minutes or until toothpick inserted into center comes out clean. Cool completely in pan on wire rack.

4. Prepare Cream Cheese Frosting. Spread frosting over bars; sprinkle with chocolate chips, if desired.

Cream Cheese Frosting: Beat 4 ounces softened cream cheese and ½ cup (1 stick) softened butter in medium bowl with electric mixer at medium-high speed about 3 minutes or until creamy. Add 2 cups powdered sugar; beat at low speed until blended. Add 1 tablespoon milk; beat at medium-high speed 2 to 3 minutes or until frosting is light and fluffy.

Pumpkin Chocolate Chip Sandwiches

Makes about 2 dozen sandwich cookies

1 cup canned pumpkin

1 package (about 16 ounces) refrigerated chocolate chip cookie dough

¾ cup all-purpose flour

½ teaspoon pumpkin pie spice*

½ cup prepared cream cheese frosting

Or substitute ¼ teaspoon ground cinnamon, ⅛ teaspoon ground ginger and pinch each ground allspice and ground nutmeg.

1. Line colander with paper towel. Place pumpkin in colander; drain about 20 minutes to remove excess moisture.

2. Let dough stand at room temperature 15 minutes. Preheat oven to 350°F. Grease cookie sheets or line with parchment paper.

3. Beat dough, pumpkin, flour and pumpkin pie spice in large bowl with electric mixer at medium speed until well blended. Drop dough by rounded teaspoonfuls 2 inches apart onto prepared cookie sheets.

4. Bake 9 to 11 minutes or until set. Cool on cookie sheets 3 minutes; remove to wire racks to cool completely.

5. Pipe or spread about 1 teaspoon frosting on flat side of half of cookies; top with remaining cookies.

Soft Pumpkin Cookies

Makes about 3½ dozen cookies

½ cup (1 stick) butter, softened

1 cup packed brown sugar

½ cup granulated sugar

1½ cups canned pumpkin

1 egg

1 teaspoon vanilla

2¼ cups all-purpose flour

1¼ teaspoons ground cinnamon

1 teaspoon baking powder

½ teaspoon baking soda

½ teaspoon salt

½ teaspoon ground nutmeg

¾ cup raisins

½ cup chopped walnuts

Powdered Sugar Glaze (recipe follows)

1. Preheat oven to 350°F.

2. Beat butter, brown sugar and granulated sugar in large bowl with electric mixer at medium speed about 2 minutes or until creamy. Add pumpkin, egg and vanilla; beat until light and fluffy. Add flour, cinnamon, baking powder, baking soda, salt and nutmeg; beat at low speed just until blended. Stir in raisins and walnuts. Drop dough by heaping tablespoonfuls 2 inches apart onto ungreased cookie sheets.

3. Bake 12 to 15 minutes or until set. Cool on cookie sheets 2 minutes; remove to wire racks to cool completely.

4. Prepare Powdered Sugar Glaze. Drizzle glaze over cookies; let stand until set. Store cookies in airtight container between layers of waxed paper.

Powdered Sugar Glaze: Combine 1 cup powdered sugar and 2 tablespoons milk in small bowl; whisk until smooth.

Pumpkin Swirl Brownies

Makes about 16 brownies

Pumpkin Swirl

4 ounces cream cheese, softened

½ cup canned pumpkin

1 egg

3 tablespoons sugar

¾ teaspoon pumpkin pie spice

Pinch salt

Brownies

½ cup (1 stick) butter

6 ounces semisweet chocolate, chopped

1 cup sugar

3 eggs

1 teaspoon vanilla

¾ cup all-purpose flour

2 tablespoons unsweetened cocoa powder

½ teaspoon salt

1. Preheat oven to 350°F. Spray 8-inch square baking pan with nonstick cooking spray or line with parchment paper.

2. For swirl, combine cream cheese, pumpkin, 1 egg, 3 tablespoons sugar, pumpkin pie spice and pinch of salt in medium bowl; beat until smooth.

3. For brownies, melt butter and chocolate in medium saucepan over low heat, stirring frequently. Remove from heat; stir in 1 cup sugar until blended. Beat in 3 eggs, one at a time, until well blended. Stir in vanilla. Add flour, cocoa and ½ teaspoon salt; stir until blended. Reserve ⅓ cup brownie batter in small bowl; spread remaining batter in prepared pan.

4. Spread pumpkin mixture evenly over brownie batter. Drop reserved brownie batter by teaspoonfuls over pumpkin layer; draw tip of knife through both batters to marbleize. (If reserved brownie batter has become very thick upon standing, microwave on LOW (30%) 20 to 30 seconds or until loosened, stirring at 10-second intervals.)

5. Bake 28 to 30 minutes or just until center is set and edges begin to pull away from sides of pan. (Toothpick will come out with fudgy crumbs.) Cool completely in pan on wire rack.

Pumpkin Oatmeal Cookies

Makes about 2 dozen cookies

1 cup all-purpose flour

1 teaspoon ground cinnamon

½ teaspoon salt

½ teaspoon ground nutmeg

¼ teaspoon baking soda

1½ cups packed brown sugar

½ cup (1 stick) butter, softened

1 egg

1 teaspoon vanilla

½ cup canned pumpkin

2 cups old-fashioned oats

1 cup dried cranberries
(optional)

1. Preheat oven to 350°F. Line cookie sheets with parchment paper.

2. Sift flour, cinnamon, salt, nutmeg and baking soda into medium bowl. Beat brown sugar and butter in large bowl with electric mixer at medium speed about 5 minutes or until light and fluffy.

3. Beat in egg and vanilla until blended. Add pumpkin; beat at low speed until blended. Add flour mixture; beat at low speed just until blended. Add oats; mix well. Stir in cranberries, if desired. Drop dough by rounded tablespoonfuls 2 inches apart onto prepared cookie sheets.

4. Bake 12 minutes or until golden brown. Cool on cookie sheets 1 minute; remove to wire racks to cool completely.

Delicious Desserts

Pumpkin Bread Pudding
Makes 2 servings

◇◇

2 slices whole wheat bread

1 cup canned pumpkin

1 egg

2 tablespoons sugar

1 teaspoon vanilla

½ teaspoon ground cinnamon, plus additional for garnish

⅛ teaspoon salt

1 tablespoon raisins

  Whipped topping (optional)

1. Preheat oven to 375°F. Lightly spray two custard cups or ramekins with nonstick cooking spray.

2. Toast bread; cut into 1-inch cubes.

3. Whisk pumpkin, egg, sugar, vanilla, ½ teaspoon cinnamon and salt in medium bowl until well blended. Fold in toasted bread cubes and raisins. Divide mixture evenly between prepared custard cups.

4. Bake 30 minutes. Serve warm with whipped topping, if desired. Garnish with additional cinnamon.

Pumpkin Mousse

Makes 6 servings

1 cup milk

1 package (4-serving size) butterscotch instant pudding and pie filling mix

1 can (15 ounces) pure pumpkin

¼ teaspoon ground cinnamon

Pinch ground ginger

Pinch ground cloves

1 container (8 ounces) whipped topping, divided

2 tablespoons chopped crystallized ginger (optional)

1. Whisk milk and pudding mix in large bowl until blended. Add pumpkin, cinnamon, ground ginger and cloves; whisk until well blended.

2. Reserve ¼ cup whipped topping for garnish. Fold remaining whipped topping into pudding mixture. Refrigerate 1 hour or until set.

3. Top mousse with dollop of reserved whipped topping just before serving; garnish with crystallized ginger.

Pumpkin Cranberry Custard

Makes 4 to 6 servings

1 can (30 ounces) pumpkin pie mix

1 can (12 ounces) evaporated milk

4 eggs, beaten

1 cup dried cranberries

Whole or crushed gingersnap cookies (optional)

Whipped cream (optional)

Slow Cooker Directions

1. Combine pumpkin pie mix, evaporated milk, eggs and cranberries in slow cooker; mix well.

2. Cover; cook on HIGH 4 to 4½ hours.

3. Serve custard with gingersnap cookies and whipped cream, if desired.

Tip: To crush gingersnap cookies, place them in a resealable food storage bag and seal the bag. Crush the cookies into coarse crumbs using a rolling pin or the back of a skillet or saucepan.

Pumpkin Panna Cotta with Raspberry Sauce

Makes 8 servings

4 teaspoons unflavored gelatin

¼ cup cold water

4 cups whipping cream, divided

¾ cup packed brown sugar

1 can (15 ounces) pure pumpkin

1 tablespoon vanilla

1 teaspoon ground cardamom

Raspberry Sauce
(recipe follows)

1. Lightly spray eight 6-ounce fluted tins or custard cups with nonstick cooking spray.

2. Sprinkle gelatin over cold water in small saucepan; let stand 5 minutes to soften. Heat over low heat until melted.

3. Combine 2 cups cream and brown sugar in medium saucepan; bring to a simmer over medium heat. Remove from heat; whisk in gelatin mixture, remaining 2 cups cream, pumpkin, vanilla and cardamom until blended. Divide mixture evenly among prepared tins. Refrigerate at least 6 hours.

4. Meanwhile, prepare Raspberry Sauce. To unmold, dip bottoms of tins briefly into hot water; invert panna cotta onto individual serving plates. Serve with sauce.

Raspberry Sauce: Press 1 (12-ounce) package thawed frozen raspberries lightly in sieve set over small saucepan to extract juice. Discard pulp. Add ¼ cup granulated sugar to saucepan; cook and stir over medium-high heat about 3 minutes or until heated through. Whisk ¾ teaspoon cornstarch into 2 tablespoons water in small bowl until smooth. Slowly whisk cornstarch mixture into raspberry mixture; bring to a boil. Cook and stir 2 minutes or until slightly thickened. Refrigerate until ready to serve.

No-Bake Pumpkin Mousse Parfaits

Makes 8 servings

2 ounces cream cheese, softened

1 can (15 ounces) pure pumpkin

¾ cup milk

1 package (4-serving size) vanilla instant pudding and pie filling mix

1 teaspoon ground cinnamon

½ teaspoon ground ginger

⅛ teaspoon ground cloves

3 cups thawed frozen whipped topping, divided

4 gingersnap cookies, crushed

1. Beat cream cheese in medium bowl with electric mixer at medium speed about 2 minutes or until smooth and creamy. Add pumpkin, milk, pudding mix, cinnamon, ginger and cloves; beat 1 minute or until well blended. Fold in 1½ cups whipped topping.

2. Spoon ¼ cup mousse into each of eight 6-ounce dessert glasses. Layer with 2 tablespoons whipped topping and ¼ cup mousse. Cover and refrigerate 1 hour.

3. Just before serving, top each parfait with remaining whipped topping and cookie crumbs.

Caramel Pumpkin Flan

Makes about 6 servings

◇◇

¾ cup sugar, divided

4 eggs

1 cup canned pumpkin

1 teaspoon ground cinnamon

¼ teaspoon salt

¼ teaspoon ground ginger

¼ teaspoon ground nutmeg

¼ teaspoon ground allspice

1 cup half-and-half

½ teaspoon vanilla

1. Preheat oven to 350°F. Heat ½ cup sugar in 8-inch skillet over medium heat until sugar is melted and golden brown, stirring constantly. Immediately pour caramel into 1-quart soufflé dish or 8-inch baking dish. Tilt dish so caramel spreads over bottom and slightly up side of dish. Let stand 10 minutes.

2. Beat eggs in large bowl with electric mixer at medium speed until frothy. Add remaining ¼ cup sugar, pumpkin, cinnamon, salt, ginger, nutmeg and allspice; beat until well blended. Add half-and-half and vanilla; beat until smooth.

3. Pour pumpkin mixture over caramel in soufflé dish. Place soufflé dish in larger baking pan; add warm water to baking pan to depth of 1½ inches.

4. Bake 45 to 50 minutes or until knife inserted into center comes out clean. Remove soufflé dish from baking pan; cool on wire rack. Cover loosely and refrigerate 6 hours or overnight.

5. To unmold, run knife around edge of soufflé dish. Cover with rimmed serving plate and invert dish; flan and caramel will slide onto plate. Cut into wedges to serve; spoon caramel over top.

Maple Pumpkin Fudge

Makes 3 pounds

2½ cups sugar

½ cup (1 stick) butter, cut into pieces

1 can (5 ounces) evaporated milk

½ cup canned pumpkin

1½ teaspoons pumpkin pie spice

1 package (about 11 ounces) white chocolate chips

1 jar (7 ounces) marshmallow creme

1 cup chopped walnuts

1½ teaspoons maple flavoring

1. Line 13×9-inch baking pan with foil, with ends of foil extending over edges of pan. Spray foil with nonstick cooking spray.

2. Combine sugar, butter, evaporated milk, pumpkin and pumpkin pie spice in large saucepan; bring to a boil over medium heat, stirring constantly. Reduce heat to medium-low; boil, stirring constantly, until mixture reaches soft-ball stage (238°F).

3. Stir in chocolate chips, marshmallow creme, walnuts and maple flavoring. Remove from heat; stir constantly until chocolate melts and fudge becomes satiny. Immediately pour into prepared pan (do not scrape side of saucepan) and spread evenly.

4. Let stand at room temperature until cool. Refrigerate until firm. Use foil to lift fudge out of pan; remove foil and cut into squares.

Pumpkin Crème Brûlée

Makes 4 servings

1 cup whipping cream

1 cup half-and-half

½ cup granulated sugar

¼ teaspoon salt

¼ teaspoon ground cinnamon

Pinch ground nutmeg
(optional)

4 egg yolks

½ cup canned pumpkin

4 tablespoons packed
brown sugar

1. Preheat oven to 300°F. Spray four 1-cup shallow ramekins or custard cups with nonstick cooking spray.

2. Combine cream, half-and-half, granulated sugar, salt, cinnamon and nutmeg, if desired, in medium saucepan; bring to a simmer over medium-high heat.

3. Beat egg yolks in medium heatproof bowl. Gradually whisk in one fourth of hot cream mixture. Slowly pour egg yolk mixture back into remaining cream mixture in saucepan, whisking constantly until slightly thickened. Remove from heat; whisk in pumpkin until well blended.

4. Pour into prepared ramekins. Place ramekins in 9-inch square baking pan. Add hot water to baking pan to depth of 1 inch.

5. Bake 45 to 55 minutes or until set. Cool ramekins in pan 30 minutes. Remove from pan; refrigerate at least 1 hour.

6. Preheat broiler. Sprinkle 1 tablespoon brown sugar evenly over each custard. Place ramekins on baking sheet. Broil 4 inches from heat 1 minute or until sugar begins to bubble and turn golden brown. Cool 15 minutes before serving.

Pumpkin Cheesecake in Pastry

Makes 6 servings

1 package frozen puff pastry shells (6 shells)

1 package (4-serving size) vanilla instant pudding and pie filling mix

1 cup milk

1 package (8 ounces) cream cheese, softened

½ (15-ounce) can pure pumpkin

⅓ cup maple syrup

2 teaspoons ground cinnamon, plus additional for garnish

1 teaspoon vanilla

¼ teaspoon ground nutmeg

¼ teaspoon ground allspice

1. Bake puff pastry shells according to package directions. Cool completely on wire rack.

2. Meanwhile, combine pudding mix, milk, cream cheese, pumpkin, maple syrup, 2 teaspoons cinnamon, vanilla, nutmeg and allspice in food processor; process until smooth. Transfer to medium bowl; cover and refrigerate until ready to serve.

3. Just before serving, remove tops of pastry shells. Spoon about ½ cup pumpkin filling into each shell; replace tops. Sprinkle with additional cinnamon.

Pumpkin Mousse Cups

Makes 8 servings

1¼ cups whipping cream, divided

1 cup canned pumpkin

⅓ cup sugar

½ teaspoon pumpkin pie spice

⅛ teaspoon salt

½ teaspoon vanilla

½ cup crushed gingersnap cookies (about 8 small gingersnaps)

1. Combine ½ cup cream, pumpkin, sugar, pumpkin pie spice and salt in small saucepan; bring to a simmer over medium heat. Reduce heat to low; simmer 15 minutes, stirring occasionally. Remove from heat; stir in vanilla. Set aside to cool to room temperature.

2. Beat remaining ¾ cup cream in medium bowl with electric mixer at high speed until soft peaks form. Gently fold 1 cup whipped cream into pumpkin mixture until well blended. Refrigerate until ready to serve.

3. Spoon heaping ¼ cup pumpkin mousse into each of eight ½-cup glasses or dessert dishes. Top with dollop of remaining whipped cream; sprinkle with crushed cookies.

Tip: Store leftover canned pumpkin in an airtight container in the refrigerator for up to 1 week or in the freezer for up to 3 months.

Pumpkin Pie Pops

Makes 6 pops

½ cup canned pumpkin pie mix

½ cup milk

¼ teaspoon vanilla

1½ cups vanilla ice cream

6 (5-ounce) paper or plastic cups or pop molds

2 containers (4 ounces each) prepared refrigerated vanilla pudding, divided

3 teaspoons packed brown sugar, divided

6 whole cinnamon sticks or pop sticks

1. Combine pumpkin pie mix, milk and vanilla in blender or food processor; blend until smooth. Add ice cream; blend until smooth. Pour 2 tablespoons mixture into each cup. Freeze 30 to 45 minutes or just until set. Cover and refrigerate remaining pumpkin mixture.

2. Combine 1 container vanilla pudding and 1½ teaspoons brown sugar in small bowl; mix well. Spoon 1 tablespoon mixture over pumpkin mixture in each cup. Freeze 30 to 45 minutes or just until set.

3. Pour 2 tablespoons reserved pumpkin mixture over pudding mixture in each cup. Freeze 30 to 45 minutes or until just set. Cover and refrigerate remaining pumpkin mixture.

4. Combine remaining 1 container pudding and 1½ teaspoons brown sugar in small bowl; mix well. Spoon 1 tablespoon mixture over pumpkin mixture in each cup. Freeze 30 to 45 minutes or just until set.

5. Pour 1 tablespoon reserved pumpkin mixture over pudding mixture in each cup. Cover top of each cup with small piece of foil. Freeze 30 to 45 minutes or just until set.

6. Gently insert cinnamon sticks through center of foil. Freeze 6 hours or until firm. To serve, remove foil and peel away paper cups or gently twist frozen pops out of plastic cups.

Slow Cooker Pumpkin Custard

Makes 6 servings

1 cup canned pumpkin

½ cup packed brown sugar

2 eggs

½ teaspoon ground ginger

½ teaspoon grated lemon peel

½ teaspoon ground cinnamon, plus additional for garnish

1 can (12 ounces) evaporated milk

Slow Cooker Directions

1. Whisk pumpkin, brown sugar, eggs, ginger, lemon peel and ½ teaspoon cinnamon in large bowl until well blended. Whisk in evaporated milk. Pour mixture into 1½-quart soufflé dish; cover tightly with foil.

2. Make foil handles.* Place soufflé dish in slow cooker. Pour water into slow cooker to come about 1½ inches from top of soufflé dish.

3. Cover; cook on LOW 4 hours. Use foil handles to lift dish from slow cooker. Sprinkle with additional cinnamon. Serve warm.

*To make foil handles, tear off three 18×3-inch strips of heavy-duty foil. Crisscross strips so they resemble spokes of a wheel. Place dish in center of foil strips; pull strips up and over dish to place in slow cooker. Leave foil strips in while cooking so dish can be easily lifted out again when cooking is complete.

Pumpkin Pie Trifle

Makes 8 to 10 servings

1 prepared angel food cake
2 cups canned pumpkin pie mix
1½ cups whipping cream
   Colored sprinkles (optional)

1. Cut cake into 1-inch cubes. Place pumpkin pie mix in medium bowl.

2. Beat cream in large bowl with electric mixer at medium-high speed until stiff peaks form.

3. Spoon one third of whipped cream into pumpkin pie mix; fold with spatula until blended. Add another third of whipped cream to pumpkin mixture; fold gently until uniform in color. Reserve remaining one third of whipped cream for garnish.

4. Layer cake cubes and pumpkin mixture in trifle dish or deep glass bowl, beginning and ending with pumpkin mixture. Garnish with reserved whipped cream and sprinkles.

Pumpkin Seed Brittle

Makes about 2 pounds

2 cups sugar

1 cup water

1 cup corn syrup

¼ teaspoon cream of tartar

¼ teaspoon salt

2 cups roasted salted
   pumpkin seeds

1 tablespoon butter,
   cut into small pieces

½ teaspoon baking soda

1. Grease two baking sheets.

2. Combine sugar, water, corn syrup, cream of tartar and salt in heavy medium saucepan; cook over medium heat until sugar dissolves and mixture comes to a boil, stirring constantly. Wash down side of saucepan with pastry brush or paper towel frequently dipped in hot water to remove sugar crystals and prevent burning.

3. Attach candy thermometer to side of saucepan, making sure bulb is submerged in sugar mixture but not touching bottom of pan. Continue to cook until mixture reaches soft-ball stage (238°F). Stir in pumpkin seeds; cook until mixture reaches 295°F.

4. Remove from heat; stir in butter and baking soda. Immediately pour hot mixture onto prepared baking sheets. Working quickly, use two forks to stretch mixture as thin as possible. Let stand until set. Break brittle into pieces; store in airtight container.

Pumpkin Ice Cream
Makes 5½ cups

¾ cup canned pumpkin

½ cup packed brown sugar

¼ cup granulated sugar

2 teaspoons ground cinnamon

1 teaspoon ground ginger

¼ teaspoon salt

1½ cups whipping cream

1 cup whole milk

1 tablespoon molasses

4 egg yolks

1 tablespoon cornstarch mixed with 1 tablespoon cold milk

1. Cook pumpkin in medium saucepan over medium heat 5 minutes, stirring frequently. Add brown sugar, granulated sugar, cinnamon, ginger and salt; cook and stir 1 minute. Whisk in cream, milk and molasses over medium-high heat; bring to a boil, stirring frequently. Remove from heat.

2. Whisk egg yolks in small bowl. Slowly whisk in ½ cup hot pumpkin mixture until blended. Slowly whisk egg yolk mixture back into saucepan in thin, steady stream. Cook over medium heat 2 minutes or until mixture is thick enough to coat back of spoon. Add cornstarch mixture; cook and stir 1 minute.

3. Set fine-mesh strainer over medium bowl. Pour pumpkin mixture through strainer into bowl, pressing with spatula to force mixture through.

4. Fill large bowl half full with cold water and ice. Place bowl with pumpkin mixture in ice bath; stir occasionally until mixture is cool.

5. Cover and refrigerate overnight or churn immediately in ice cream maker according to manufacturer's directions. Pack ice cream into freezer container; freeze until firm.

Gingered Pumpkin Custard

Makes 6 servings

¾ cup sugar

2 eggs

1½ teaspoons ground cinnamon

½ teaspoon salt

½ teaspoon ground nutmeg

1 can (15 ounces) pure pumpkin

1¼ cups half-and-half

3 tablespoons finely chopped candied ginger, divided

Sweetened whipped cream (optional)

1. Preheat oven to 375°F. Place six 8-ounce ramekins or custard cups on baking sheet.

2. Whisk sugar, eggs, cinnamon, salt and nutmeg in medium bowl until blended. Add pumpkin and half-and-half; whisk until well blended. Stir in 2 tablespoons ginger. Pour into prepared ramekins.

3. Bake 35 to 40 minutes or until knife inserted into centers comes out clean. Cool on wire rack at least 20 minutes before serving. Serve warm or at room temperature with whipped cream, if desired. Sprinkle with remaining 1 tablespoon ginger.

Variation: To make one large dish of custard instead of individual servings, pour the custard mixture into a greased 8-inch or 1½-quart baking dish. Bake 45 minutes or until a knife inserted into the center comes out clean.

Pumpkin Spice Smoothie »

Makes 4 servings

2½ cups vanilla frozen yogurt
1 cup canned pumpkin
1 cup cubed or crushed ice
2 tablespoons packed
   brown sugar
1 tablespoon honey
1 teaspoon pumpkin pie spice
½ teaspoon ground nutmeg

Combine frozen yogurt, pumpkin, ice, brown sugar, honey, pumpkin pie spice and nutmeg in blender; blend until smooth. Serve immediately.

Pumpkin Pie Milk Shakes

Makes 4 servings

1 cup canned pumpkin pie mix
1 cup milk
½ teaspoon vanilla
4 cups vanilla ice cream
4 graham cracker squares
   Whipped cream (optional)
1 graham cracker square,
   broken into pieces
   (optional)

Combine pumpkin pie mix, milk and vanilla in blender; blend until smooth. Add ice cream; blend until smooth. Add 4 graham cracker squares; pulse until small chunks remain. Garnish with whipped cream and graham cracker pieces.

Slow Cooker Pumpkin Bread Pudding

Makes 8 servings

2 cups whole milk

½ cup plus 2 tablespoons butter, divided

1 cup canned pumpkin

3 eggs

1 cup packed dark brown sugar, divided

1 tablespoon ground cinnamon

2 teaspoons vanilla

½ teaspoon ground nutmeg

¼ teaspoon salt

16 slices cinnamon raisin bread, torn in small pieces (8 cups total)

½ cup whipping cream

2 tablespoons bourbon (optional)

Slow Cooker Directions

1. Spray inside of 3½- to 4-quart slow cooker with nonstick cooking spray.

2. Combine milk and 2 tablespoons butter in medium microwavable bowl; microwave on HIGH 2 minutes or until very hot.

3. Whisk pumpkin, eggs, ½ cup brown sugar, cinnamon, vanilla, nutmeg and salt in large bowl until well blended. Whisk in milk mixture until blended. Add bread cubes; toss to coat. Transfer to slow cooker.

4. Cover; cook on HIGH 2 hours or until knife inserted into center comes out clean. Turn off heat. Uncover; let stand 15 minutes.

5. Combine remaining ½ cup butter, ½ cup brown sugar and cream in small saucepan; bring to a boil over high heat, stirring frequently. Remove from heat. Stir in bourbon, if desired. Spoon bread pudding into individual bowls; top with sauce.

Metric Conversion Chart

VOLUME MEASUREMENTS (dry)

1/8 teaspoon = 0.5 mL
1/4 teaspoon = 1 mL
1/2 teaspoon = 2 mL
3/4 teaspoon = 4 mL
1 teaspoon = 5 mL
1 tablespoon = 15 mL
2 tablespoons = 30 mL
1/4 cup = 60 mL
1/3 cup = 75 mL
1/2 cup = 125 mL
2/3 cup = 150 mL
3/4 cup = 175 mL
1 cup = 250 mL
2 cups = 1 pint = 500 mL
3 cups = 750 mL
4 cups = 1 quart = 1 L

VOLUME MEASUREMENTS (fluid)

1 fluid ounce (2 tablespoons) = 30 mL
4 fluid ounces (1/2 cup) = 125 mL
8 fluid ounces (1 cup) = 250 mL
12 fluid ounces (1 1/2 cups) = 375 mL
16 fluid ounces (2 cups) = 500 mL

WEIGHTS (mass)

1/2 ounce = 15 g
1 ounce = 30 g
3 ounces = 90 g
4 ounces = 120 g
8 ounces = 225 g
10 ounces = 285 g
12 ounces = 360 g
16 ounces = 1 pound = 450 g

DIMENSIONS

1/16 inch = 2 mm
1/8 inch = 3 mm
1/4 inch = 6 mm
1/2 inch = 1.5 cm
3/4 inch = 2 cm
1 inch = 2.5 cm

OVEN TEMPERATURES

250°F = 120°C
275°F = 140°C
300°F = 150°C
325°F = 160°C
350°F = 180°C
375°F = 190°C
400°F = 200°C
425°F = 220°C
450°F = 230°C

BAKING PAN SIZES

Utensil	Size in Inches/Quarts	Metric Volume	Size in Centimeters
Baking or Cake Pan (square or rectangular)	8×8×2	2 L	20×20×5
	9×9×2	2.5 L	23×23×5
	12×8×2	3 L	30×20×5
	13×9×2	3.5 L	33×23×5
Loaf Pan	8×4×3	1.5 L	20×10×7
	9×5×3	2 L	23×13×7
Round Layer Cake Pan	8×1½	1.2 L	20×4
	9×1½	1.5 L	23×4
Pie Plate	8×1¼	750 mL	20×3
	9×1¼	1 L	23×3
Baking Dish or Casserole	1 quart	1 L	—
	1½ quart	1.5 L	—
	2 quart	2 L	—